DID MAN
JUST HAPPEN?

DID MAN
JUST HAPPEN?

by
W. A. CRISWELL
Pastor, First Baptist Church, Dallas, Texas
Author of *These Issues We Must Face*

ZONDERVAN PUBLISHING HOUSE
GRAND RAPIDS   MICHIGAN

First printing — 1957
Second printing — 1963
Third printing — 1965
Fourth printing — 1966
Fifth printing — 1967

DEDICATION

To my
TEEN-AGE CHAPEL CHOIR
*who listened so intently to
these messages and who add
so much to our early Sunday
morning services*

FOREWORD

These addresses on the creation of man were delivered extemporaneously and without notes. I have always preached that way — without notes — and it would have been a most unusual thing to my congregation if I had suddenly changed when I came to the twenty-sixth verse of the first chapter of Genesis. For, you see, these messages are not impersonal, scientific dissertations on some removed and recondite subject; they are, rather, a marshaling together of the very truths and verities of God gathered throughout this whole world in confirmation of the marvelous revelation disclosed in the opening chapters of the Bible. The whole after-story of the plan of redemption turns to dust and ashes if man is not a fallen creature, made in the likeness and image of God, and whose only hope is found in the restoration through the atoning grace of our Lord Jesus Christ.

It was the young people of our church who took these addresses down and so earnestly asked that they be published. They are printed here as they were delivered: not in the rounded language of the arm-chair philosopher but in the hot, ardent words of the pulpit. If I were to re-write them I would change much of the sentence structure. The people, however, said they wanted them just as they heard them; so here they are, word for word, thunder and all.

I wish I could have known the late and lamented Harry Rimmer. Of all the multitude of books I read, his volumes helped me the most. One of the most interesting stories I ever read is his account of the "Nebraska Man," repeated in the chapter on the hoaxes of anthropology.

The good Lord keep us in love with the truth and stedfast in the faith, now and forever. Amen.

— W. A. CRISWELL

Pastor's Study
First Baptist Church
Dallas, Texas
April 15, 1957

CONTENTS

THE CREATION OF MAN —
GOD OR GORILLA

Chapter I

THE CREATION OF MAN— GOD OR GORILLA

In the first chapter of Genesis, the twenty-sixth through the twenty-eighth verses, we read an account of the creation of man:

> And God said, Let us make man in our image, after our likeness: and let them have dominion over the fish of the sea, and over the fowl of the air, and over the cattle, and over all the earth, and over every creeping thing that creepeth upon the earth. So God created man in his own image, in the image of God created he him; male and female created he them. And God blessed them, and God said unto them, Be fruitful, and multiply, and replenish the earth, and subdue it: and have dominion over the fish of the sea, and over the fowl of the air, and over every living thing that moveth upon the earth.

There is an observable fact that anyone can see anywhere, anytime, and that phenomenon is this: In every way and in all ways, a man is distinct from a beast, God said so. True science says so. In bone, in blood, in flesh, in cells, in mind, in soul, in spirit, a man is distinct from an animal.

For example, a man walks erect. There is no other animal that stands up and walks erect. The anthropoid rumbles and rushes through the jungle on all fours. When he seats himself he does so ludicrously and uncomfortably. And he cannot stand up and walk erect like a man.

A man also differs from a beast in his countenance. The light of intelligence is in his face and in his eyes. One of the most beautiful passages in the New Testament is this: "For God, who commanded the light to shine out of darkness, hath shined in our hearts, to give the light of the knowledge of the glory of God in the face of Jesus Christ." The light of the knowledge of the glory of God is in the face, in the countenance of man. No beast, no animal has such a countenance. The intelligence of God is in a man's face.

A man also differs from an animal in his osteological framework, in the bone structure of his body. For example, a man has a hand. No other being has this marvelous gift of God. Only a man has a thumb in apposition to his fingers. An anthropoid will have a big toe in apposition to his other toes, but a man's foot is made for walking. An anthropoid has no thumb in apposition to his fingers. Only a man has a hand. And that miraculous gift of God enables him to handle a tool and to do things with all the multifarious instruments his mind has devised. The fin of a fish, the paw of a lion, the hoof of a horse, the claw of a bird — but only a man has a hand.

A man differs from a beast in his mind, in his reason and in his inventive genius, too.

Did you ever try teaching geology to an elephant?

Did you ever try teaching astronomy to an eagle?

Did you ever try teaching theology to a dog?

Yet the most primitive savage in the farthest, deepest jungle can learn all three. A man differs from a beast in his mind, in his intelligence, in his ability to reason and to think.

Last, a man differs from a beast in his soul, in his spirit, in the divine image God breathed into his bodily frame. How beautifully does the Bible express it when it says: "And the Lord God formed man of the dust of the ground, and breathed into his nostrils the breath of life; and man became a living soul." No other beast, no other animal has a soul, has a spirit like a man. A man has moral consciousness, the ability to know God and to think

God's thoughts after him. Man is moral, made in the image of God and he is conscious of his Creator. Professor Townsend of Boston University once said that, "Except for a mind endowed with a conscience at the beginning, and with which organic evolution has nothing to do, and had not religion, especially the Jewish and the Christian faiths, with their inspiring and uplifting power come to the aid of the human race, mankind long since would have disappeared from the face of the earth."

Now we have our facts before us. We have the observable phenomena around us. The man is distinct from the beast.

THE TWO EXPLANATIONS

How then shall we explain that demonstrable fact?

There are two explanations. The first is the one we find from the first and second chapters of the Book of Genesis. It is this: By fiat, possible only to an omnipotent and all powerful God, God created man miraculously, marvelously, wonderfully.

The Lord God made something out of nothing or caused to come into existence something that had no previous existence. God created man and breathed into his nostrils that breath of life by which he became a living soul.

The record says that God did not create man a primitive savage, but that He created him full grown with all of his faculties. Immediately after the creation of man, the intelligent Adam named all the beasts of the field and all the fowls of the earth. He was a man perfect in moral life, in intellectual life, in physical life. His body and his mind expressed the likeness and the image of God.

From that beautiful and holy and perfect estate, the man and his wife fell because of sin. And they fell to a degradation lower than some of the animals of the fields, from which depth of sin they would never have been able to deliver themselves. However, the Lord God promised a Deliverer. In the seed of the woman the fallen man can be transformed into the image of Christ, and the Tree of Life and the paradise of heaven can be restored to him. Man was created perfect, created in the image of God, created by the word of the Lord. Iniquity marred that creation. That is the record of the Bible. That is one explanation of the observable phenomena we see all around us.

The other explanation is called a hypothesis, a theory; that is, a supposition, an overt and admitted guess. There are those who seek to explain the phenomenon of a man by leaving God out and making the man a product of a mechanistic and impersonal universe. That theoretical explanation of the presence of a man is called the evolutionary hypothesis.

It is this: Somewhere there came into existence a primordial protozoon like an amoeba, a little animalcule, a speck of protoplasm, and from that animalcule, through endless and infinite transitional forms, there developed, there evolved, the man who now dominates the birds of the air, the fish of the sea and the beasts of the land.

I could not state the theory better than from Charles Darwin in the tremendous volume he published, entitled *Origin of the Species.* On page 523 of that famous book, Darwin says: "Analogy would lead me to the belief that all animals and plants are descended from some one prototype. All organisms start from a common origin, from some such low and intermediate forms both animals and plants may have been developed. All the organic beings which have ever lived on the earth may be descended from some one primordial form." This is the conclusion in the latter part of the book.

In my own words, somewhere, somehow a speck of protoplasmic substance came into existence, so small that it could not have been seen by the unaided powers of the eye. And through the generations from that one protoplasmic speck, there developed, there evolved, all the forms of life in the animal world, all the forms of life in the vegetable world. All the forms of life we see today have evolved from that one common speck of substance.

It is admittedly a breath-taking and overwhelming theory. It is stupendous! If a man gasps at the creation story in Genesis, how must he gasp in amazement at the evolutionary hypothesis, the evolving of all the forms of life that we now see, through endless numbers of transitional forms. It is an amazing theory. And the evolutionists themselves are an amazing group of people. To my surprise, I have found that the only thing they have in common is this first assumption. When they go beyond the first supposition, there are as many evolutionary theories as there are evolutionists. Each man has his own guess. Each man has his own hypothesis. Each man has his own theory. The only thing they have in common is that they all agree that all of life began in that one primordial cell.

THE AMAZING ACCEPTANCE OF THE THEORY OF EVOLUTION

Now, to my amazement, to my wonder, that theory, that hypothesis, has been generally received by the entire intellectual, scholastic world. They hardly question it. If you do, surely you must not have studied, you must not have read books, you must not have been to school at all. For every man of science and every man of intellectual stature takes for granted this explanation, mechanistic and material, of the development of the forms of life that we see in the world today.

It is astonishing how an unproved hypothesis should have come to be received as the fact of science itself. For example, this is a quotation from a textbook in one of our public schools: "Man and ape represent each a distinct species, equally descended from a common prototype. This generalized human simian [the Latin word for ape is *simia,* the Greek word for ape is *pithekos,* and when you see those combinations like pithecanthropus and simian they are taken from the Latin and Greek words meaning ape] ancestor was the remote precursor of man and lived in Miocene times, say a million years before *pithecanthropus erectus.* His life was probably arboreal (lived in trees) until the increasing cold climate drove him into caves."

Again, here is the beginning of a book on the origin and evolution of life. "In this review, we need not devote any time or space to any fresh arguments to the truth of evolution. The demonstration of evolution as a living law of nature is the greatest intellectual achievement of the Nineteenth Century. Evolution has outgrown the rank of a theory."

This is the beginning of an article in *Life* magazine on the living fossils of Australia . . . (speaking of kangaroos) "marsupials in Australia live on the last refuge evolution has left them." Then the article continues with the story of those marsupials, saying that they are descendants of the earliest mammals to evolve from reptiles. It does not argue the point. That is the basis of all the explanation of life. Just take it for granted. Never say that it is someone's wild imagination, never say that it is someone's hypothetical guesswork. It is just a fact. Animals are evolved from reptiles. The article says the higher mammals, more intelligent and more aggressive, evolved on other continents. It does not question it. That is just one of the facts of life. Then, the resulting evolution there in Australia produced the strange animals shown in these pictures.

Well pastor, why do you question it?

Why can't you be at least a theistic evolutionist?

Many, many, I suppose more than anyone ever realizes, of the great theologians and leaders of the church today are theistic evolutionists. That is, they say it does not

matter to us how God created man. They would just as
soon believe God created man from one protoplasmic speck
and evolved him up to where he is now, as to believe God
created man according to the Biblical account.

Darwin, in his *Origin of the Species,* asks the same
question. He says, "I see no reason why the views given
in this volume should shock the religious feeling of anyone. A celebrated minister of the Gospel has written to
me, 'I have gradually learned to see that it is as noble a
conception of the Deity to believe that God created a
few original forms capable of self development as it is
to believe that God created man like it says in the Bible.' "

Well, why can't you be like that "celebrated minister"
and be a theistic evolutionist?

There are three reasons:

I am not and cannot be a theistic evolutionist or a
materialistic evolutionist, or any other kind of evolutionist because first, the theory is not factual, it is not
biologically true, it is not scientifically correct or demonstrable. Any man who loves truth and who has given his
life to the fact and the revelation of God naturally recoils
from such a thing as the evolutionary hypothesis.

The evolutionist says that by the facts of biology, by
the facts of embryology, by the facts of paleontology,
by the facts of anthropology, he can demonstrate the truth
of evolution. We are going to take the facts of biology,
embryology, paleontology and anthropology and show that
there is not a fact in this world that can be demonstrated,
not one, not in any of those sciences, that will substantiate
the evolutionary hypothesis.

WHERE DID LIFE COME FROM?

The second reason why I am not an evolutionary theist
is this: The evolutionary hypothesis has no explanation
for any of the great, ultimate questions of life, things that
I really want to know.

Where did that speck of protoplasm come from in the first place? And where did the water come from to nurture the speck? How did it get there in that great, vast void of space? Who did it? The evolutionary hypothesis solves no ultimate questions at all.

Does evolution have an answer? The best answer evolutionists can give is an article that most of you read in the daily newspapers, entitled, "New Guesses Made On How Life Began." The article is from an address made before the American Association for the Advancement of Science. It says that when this earth was covered with poisonous gases, possibly, there came a bolt of lightning through those gases, possibly, and made a combination of chemicals that fell into the ocean, possibly, made amino acid, possibly, and in the body structure of life one finds amino acids. That is the present best guess about the origin of life.

Could a man feed himself on the shucks and husks of that? Where did the lightning come from, and the water in the ocean and the earth and the gases? Is there any answer? No, all is dark and void, soundless, purposeless. Joseph Le Conte said: "If life did once arise spontaneously, from any lower forms, physical or chemical by natural process, the conditions necessary for so extraordinary a change could hardly be expected to occur just once in the history of the earth. Yet they are now not only improbable but unimaginable." How did that happen just one time, just one time? Even Huxley admitted, looking back through the prodigious ages of the past, "I find no record of the beginnings of life and therefore I am devoid of any means of forming a definite conclusion as to the conditions of its appearance."

Where did life come from? The evolutionist says there was a time in this world when there was no life. Science says there was a time on this earth when there was no life. God's Book says there was a time on this earth when there was no life.

The evolutionist says it came of itself. But spontaneous generation has never been seen, cannot be produced, is not producible. Then where did it come from? The Bible says God created it.

That leads to my last avowal.

Why are you not a theist evolutionist?

I have said it is not scientifically factual, not demonstrable. I have said it offers no explanations for the great and ultimate questions of life. And the third reason is this: It is wrong, it is not right spiritually. You have to make a choice. You cannot ride two horses in opposite directions. The Bible and the evolutionary hypothesis say two entirely different things.

The Bible presents a world created in the hand of God. The Bible presents a personal Deity, through whose infinite power all of these things were made and devised and formed. The theory of evolution says that all of these things came through a materialistic, impersonal action process, for which process proponents of the theory can give no explanation. Impersonally, mechanically, these things just happened, they came to pass, and resulted in the marvelous phenomena you see today.

We must believe one or the other. Even God Himself cannot deny Himself and God Himself cannot work on two opposite principles. The Bible says man was created perfect and walked in the Garden of Eden with all the faculties he possesses today, and he fell and went down. The theory of evolution says he started as a little primordial cell and has been coming up and up and up ever since. The ideas are diametrically opposite.

What of this question of sin? According to the Bible, sin was a moral transgression of the law of God. What is sin in evolution? Sin is nothing but the drag of our ancestry, the stumbling upward. Evolution violates the whole Word of God, the atonement of Christ, the preaching of the gospel message of Jesus. It is nothing.

I have never seen a theologian or a philosopher who could believe the Bible and at the same time believe the evolutionary hypothesis. The two are opposite. They are in one direction or the other, and we choose between.

In the day it can be demonstrated that life came of spontaneous generation without God; in the day it can be demonstrated that there was no God in the creation of man, but he evolved upward by accident; in that day, my fellow religionists and I ought quietly to fold our tents and silently steal away.

Well, preacher, are you expecting to resign your pulpit?

Are you expecting to lay down your Bible?

Are you expecting to quit preaching the Gospel?

No, because I have already found to my heart's assurance that the hand that wrote the Book is the same hand that wrote His name across the sky and in the humblest little insect whose silver wings reflect a glory of the sun which shines upon him.

This is our introduction, and it shall be our purpose, in succeeding addresses, to show, not by the theories, but by the facts of biology, of embryology, of paleontology, of anthropology, of anatomy, the creative master workmanship of God Who loved us and Who made us and gave Himself for us.

CHAPTER 2

THE WITNESS OF BIOLOGY

THE WITNESS OF BIOLOGY

So God created man in his own image, in the image of God created he him: male and female created he them (Gen. 1:27).

It is an astounding thing that in the passing of time, men have come to accept the theory of evolution as being true without scrutiny, without apology, without defense. It has come to be an accepted doctrine in the scholastic, in the academic and even in the ecclesiastical world.

For example, in *Time* magazine there was a recent article that began with this sentence: "For a long time, it looked as if the battle against evolution was about over." What does *Time* mean when it says "it looked as if the battle against evolution was about over"? Does it mean that the battle against evolution was going against the doctrine and the theory? No, what the magazine means is that the battle against evolution is "about over" in that the battle has been lost. Men have come to conclude that evolution is a full and acceptable theory of the origin and the development of all the forms and phenomena of life.

Another instance of that: Recently I received a gracious note from the illustrious federal judge, Judge T. Whitfield Davidson. The great federal jurist sent me a copy of a lesson he had delivered to his Sunday school class, entitled "The Faith of Our Fathers." On page fifteen of that lesson the judge taught his Sunday school class, he said, referring to Mr. Darwin and his *Origin of the Species*: "His conclusions have been universally accepted and he who does not respect them is not considered even literate."

But just for the interest of it, may I continue with what the judge has to say about Mr. Darwin. I quote again:

> However, the basis of the conclusion upon which he founded his theory is but little above a surmise. Under the rules of circumstantial evidence, he could not establish any fact before a judge and a jury. If his theory and teaching be correct, then well; if incorrect, he has done Christianity a great disservice. History reveals man of 6,000 years ago the same as of today. If the apes have not produced a new man in 6,000 years, how do we know they ever did? The ape is still with us. He is in the zoo. He is in the jungle. Why shouldn't he give us another specimen of his offspring? A later edition might be an improvement upon the first.

Evolution has become an accepted theory and explanation of the phenomenon and development of life everywhere. In Henry Fairfield Osborn's book, *The Origin and Evolution of Life*, this late scientist wrote: "In this review, we need not devote any time or space to any fresh arguments for the truth of evolution. The demonstration of evolution as a living law of nature is the greatest intellectual achievement of the Nineteenth Century. Evolution has outgrown the rank of a theory."

Yet in that same book, and in the face of what he had just said, Prof. Osborn devoted the first half to proving that the origin and evolution of life is impossible without spontaneous generation. He apparently seemed to think that spontaneous generation of life must be proved before anything of evolution can become anything but a theory. And yet the most impossible thing of proof in this world is the theory of the spontaneous generation of life!

This monstrous lie of the development of life through evolutionary processes, I say, has come to be the accepted theory in circles scholastic, academic, scientific and ecclesiastical! It is a denial of God; it is a denial of the human soul; it makes man a beast; it empties the world of all those holy things God reveals in His Book! And yet it has become the accepted doctrine of intellectual circles all around us.

It is the proposal of this address to prove that the facts of biology scorn and repudiate the theory and the hypothesis of evolution. The analogies we see all around us of change and development in life and in nature do not support evolution; they contradict it.

DISPLAYS IN SMITHSONIAN INSTITUTION

Many of us have visited the Smithsonian Institution, and in that institution we found phases of development like this: Here will be a little two-cylinder gas buggy, and then all through the following years, from the rudimentary form of that little gas buggy, one will see the automobile develop until it reaches its present stage of style and beauty.

Here, too, we find demonstrated the evolutionary forms of the telephone and the telegraph, of the radio and other scientific instruments, from those first beginnings until their glorious consummation now.

Sometimes we use the word evolution in referring to these developments, but the theorists of this doctrine do not agree with that meaning and with that definition at all. When we refer to the evolution of the automobile in its development, we are referring to the development that has come to pass from the application of the genius of mind and the guiding hand of man. Each of these developments in the automobile and the radio and the television is the expression of a man's thoughts and a man's mind and a man's guiding genius.

Were it suggested to you that these developments came by spontaneous generation, were it suggested to you that these developments came because of powers and laws inherent in that little gas buggy itself, you would say, "That's preposterous! That's impossible!" And yet that is exactly the sense in which the theorists use the word "evolution." With regard to inorganic evolution, they refer to the development of inorganic matter from one form to another. And with regard to the development of organic evolution, they refer to the development of life from one form into another.

You say it is preposterous for a man to believe that an automobile or a radio could develop of itself into anything else. It has to have a mind and a genius guiding that development.

If you were to take that two-cylinder gas buggy and put it out on a vacant lot and there of its own self, of resident powers inherent within it, it began to develop and evolve into all of the beautiful automobiles we see today, that would not be evolution. Not yet, because it is still an automobile. But if, while you observe that thing on the lot, it began to sprout wings, it began to develop into something else, say a jet bomber or a DC-7 and flew away, that would be evolution!

You say, "Why, that's preposterous and insensible!"

That is no more preposterous and no more insensible than for a man to say that out of nothing something came, and that out of something an amoeba came, and out of that amoeba a fish came, and out of that fish an amphibian came, and out of that amphibian a reptile came, and out of that reptile a bird came, and out of that bird a mammal came, and out of that mammal a man came. They are both preposterous and ridiculous and absurd! I say there is no substantiating fact for either of them, demonstrable or observable, anywhere, any time, any place!

Mutation, variation and varieties are seen on every hand. Here are some roses, a pink rose, a yellow rose, a red rose, and a white rose, all kinds of roses. Those roses are mutative. They are varieties. There are chickens, all kinds of chickens, little chickens and big chickens, black chickens and red chickens, yellow chickens and speckled chickens, all kinds of chickens. But they are mutative. They are varieties of a creature within their species. There is mutation everywhere, but there is transmutation nowhere, any time or any place! When that rose develops and develops and progresses and progresses until it becomes something other than a rose, say an orange tree, that is transmutation! That is evolution! When that chicken develops to the place where it is no longer a chicken but is something else, say a cow, a horse or a rabbit, then that is transmutation and that is evolution!

The evolution hypothesis is unable to account for any of the vitally differing phenomena that we see in all the world around us. Here is nothing, nothing, and here is something. How do you explain that something that is in nothing, a "thing" in a great void of space around it?

The evolutionary hypothesis says that something evolved. It evolved out of what? "Well, I don't know." It evolved from where? "Well, I don't know." Inevitably, the answer of evolution to any vital question or to any vitally differing phenomenon is, "I don't know."

Herbert Spencer of the nineteenth century thought to apply the arguments of organic evolution, proposed by Darwin, to inorganic matter, to the evolution of all the universe. But when he got back to the great crux of the problem, he had to say: "I have to begin with a first great unknowable cause."

The Latin proverb is still true: "Out of nothing, nothing comes."

Between space that is void and empty, nothingness, and the slightest speck of dust, there is a tremendous gulf that evolution cannot begin to explain. And evolution, as it is helpless before an explanation of the beginning of matter, is no less helpless in an explanation of the beginning of life and the forms of life.

A World Teeming with Life

This world teems with life. It is everywhere. There is life riding on every speck of dust. There is life in every drop of moisture. There is life in the air we breathe. There is life in the depths of the ocean. There is life in the depths of the deepest caverns. There is life under the hot, boiling Sahara sun. There is life in the smallest pool of the desert. There is life everywhere.

How do you account for the presence of life in this world?

In my reading, I have only been able to find three different guesses of those who are evolutionists. The first guess is this:

1. Some of the evolutionists say that life began on this planet by a germ riding on a meteor or some other matter that fell down to earth. But that fails to solve the problem. It merely shifts it from one place to another. Instead of accounting for life here, we have to account for it on some other planet. How did it come to pass that there was life on the other planet or the other sun? This theory is not the answer.

2. The second theory of evolution is that life came to pass because of spontaneous generation. That is the thing our boys and girls in high school come to me with. They say, "My biology teacher and my science teacher said life began in a green scum." I am surprised at that and amazed and astounded. For I thought that in the latter part of the nineteenth century Louis Pasteur demonstrated for all time that there is no such thing as the spontaneous generation of life.

I can take a piece of straw or a piece of grass and put it in water and soon that stagnant water is teeming with all kinds of small animalcules, but every one of them was born because of the presence of life on the grass, and because of the presence of life in the water. They grew from cells or spores or seeds or eggs.

Pasteur demonstrated that there is no such thing in this earth as life coming from anything but antecedent life. If a thing is sterile, it is sterile forever! There has never been any demonstrable proof that spontaneous generation has ever occurred or will ever occur! Some of the greatest scientists say it is unthinkable and unimaginable!

3. The last guess is one that I read now in magazines and newspapers. The third guess on the part of the evolutionists about how life began is this: They say it came about accidentally. For example, a great flash of lightning passed through the gaseous vapors that envelop this earth and created a life that fell down into the ocean and began to grow and evolve until finally the man emerged.

That guess reminds me of a little passage I read recently in the *Reader's Digest.* Quoting Professor Edwin Conklin, the great Princeton University biologist, it said: "The probability of life beginning from accident is comparable to the probability of the unabridged dictionary resulting from an explosion in a printing factory." Just about as likely!

Not only is the hypothesis, the theory or the guess of evolution — whatever you want to call it — unable to explain any of the differing phenomena we see around us, but there is also another thing to be earnestly considered. The fixedness, the fixity of the species is a rebuke to, and a repudiation of, the theory of evolution! A species is a solid, unbreakable unit in the organic world! God made it so. There may be varieties in the species. There may be mutation in the species. There may be change and development in the species. But the species itself is unbreakable! It has never been demonstrated that the limits of a species have ever been passed. That is according to the law of God. The Lord God said that the fowls of the air and the fish of the sea and the living creatures on the earth shall bring forth after their kind and there is never any deviation from that law!

Wherever a life form is, it gives birth to a progeny after its kind. There is no exception to that, neither in geological time, nor in primeval time, nor in historical time, nor in observable time, nor in contemporary time. The fixity of the species is a blind alley up which evolution comes to a dead end! It is a Rubicon that evolution cannot cross!

There is something good about that, something nice about that. Someone sent me a cartoon showing two monkeys hanging in a tree. One of the monkeys is scratching his head and the other is nursing a baby monkey in her arms. The mama monkey says to the papa monkey, "Thank goodness he's normal; I was afraid of evolution!"

But may we demonstrate that. The fixity and the fixedness of species, the law of God that binds them in an unbreakable unit, is a demonstrable, observable fact, anywhere, everywhere, in every geologic age and in observable time.

Let us take for example the infusoria, those animalcules, those tiny specks of protoplasm, those unicellular animals that are in profusion over this world in uncounted billions and trillions of numbers. They are everywhere. Now, a protozoologist can look at these creatures with a microscope, and they are as different to him as a horse from a cow, an ox from a pig, and a donkey from a chicken. Altogether different. In many, many ways they differ — in their locomotion, in their digestive systems, in their breathing habits, and in their manner of giving birth to their young. They are amazingly different, and yet in one category and in one place, they are all exactly alike. That is this: Every one of the one-cell animals gives birth to progeny exactly like itself. There is no exception.

These little multiplying creatures of God can be observed by the billions and billions and billions, through the thousands and thousands of their generations. Yet their progeny are all exactly alike. The paramecium, after a thousand times a thousand generations, is still the same paramecium. The amoeba, after a thousand times a thousand generations, is still the same amoeba. They never change. They never evolve. They never pass from one to the other. They are exactly the same as God made them in the beginning.

"Ah, pastor, now wait a minute," you say. "You have to realize that we have only seen these little teeming animals since the invention of the microscope. You have to remember that in the geologic ages we didn't have microscopes."

In the beginning of life there was what is now called the Paleozoic age, millions and millions of years ago. And in the Paleozoic age, there was a Silurian period, and in that period there were little coral working on the bed of the ocean. The fossilized life of that Silurian period can be seen today, and after the passing of these millions and millions of years, the coral today that works on the bed of the ocean is exactly the same, identical to the Silurian period coral that worked in the dawn of life. It has never changed. It has never evolved. God set it that way.

All of these life forms are contemporary around us. It is sheer supposition, it is sheer postulation, to say that an amoeba is older than a horse or any one of God's other creatures. If a man came from an anthropoid and a worm from an amoeba, why is it we do not see any of those vast so-called transitional forms either in contemporary life today or in any geologic age?

It is an astounding fact that out of the uncounted millions and billions and trillions of transitional forms that were supposed to have been between the development of an amoeba and a man, there is not one seen today. Nor is there one found in geological life or time or age or history. Not one. Why don't the evolutionists produce just one and say, "Here is an example of a transitional form where one species transmuted into another species"? It cannot be found; it cannot be produced; it cannot be demonstrated. God fixed those species in solid, unbreakable units, and they are there according to the law of the almighty God.

Mr. Etheridge, the great, eminent paleontologist of the British Museum, once said: "There is not one iota of proof in this great museum for the transmutation of species." Not one, not one. There is no such thing. The fixedness of the species is an affront to, a repudiation of, and a rebuke to the hypothesis of evolution.

Evolution cannot account for the presence of matter in this world, or how something came out of nothing. Evolution cannot account for the beginning of life, how life came out of that something, out of matter. Nor can evolution account for this marvelous, mysterious, physic, thing we call soul, spirit, the play of thought, the play of mind.

THE MIND AND SOUL OF MAN

What does evolution say concerning the development of mind and where it came from?

In the beginning of life, we are told, atoms of carbon and atoms of nitrogen and atoms of hydrogen, along with a little sulphur and a little phosphorus and a few other things, got together and life emerged.

That explains nothing. That is just a jugglery of words.

Wherever we meet life, wherever life emerges, there we meet a set of properties and qualities that are altogether non-special and non-metrical and non-measurable. We meet qualities that are in a different category altogether.

Wherever there is life, for example, there is purpose. There is accommodation to circumstances. There is choice. How would you say that purpose has shape or color or density or weight? Would you say that purpose is round or square? Just what density does it have? These qualities are altogether in a different category from physical categories.

In the seas of the world there are uncounted billions and billions of microscopic animals. Some of them are called radiolaria and others diatoms. Some of them build exquisite little houses out of molecules of chalk or lime, others out of flint or silica. What I want to know is this: How is it that one of these little animalcules knows how to choose between a molecule of chalk and a molecule of silica? Who taught that little speck of life to distinguish in that sea water the difference between a molecule of this or that substance to build his house in his own way?

"Why, pastor, we have an answer for that," you say. "Darwin taught them that; Einstein taught them that." Or another says, "No, I taught them that; I did it!"

For you to do that is just as likely and just as supposable as to say that such qualities came from physical properties. God taught the animal how to choose between a molecule of chalk and a molecule of silica in order to build its tiny house!

Did you ever ponder the wisdom of the ant? And yet all those properties of preparation and wisdom and choice in the ant are nothing but the expression of tiny bits of living matter called nerves or ganglia. The central ganglion of an ant, by which it directs all its life, that little speck of living matter, is not as big as the tenth point of the size of a pinhead! And yet ants will have splendid social ways and live in fine colonies, and they will divide their functions between queens and nurses and soldiers, and watchmen and scavengers and gatherers of food, and they will prepare for their young, and they will prepare their food for a rainy day. In all ways they are altruistic and wise.

How did that wisdom get in that little blob of living matter? Who put it there?

There is a quality in the property that makes up living matter that is far beyond any quality that physical matter presents. It is something else; it is nonmaterial and non-measurable.

The evolutionist has one other thing to say about the development of mind and that is this: In the evolution of life, he says, in the evolving upward of life, qualities of mind were developed because of the animal's fight for survival. It is the survival of the fittest. For you see, the theorist says, the one who was smart enough to provide for his young and smart enough to provide for his home and smart enough to provide for the future, was the one who lived and survived. The others died.

The evolutionist has no explanation for where that mind came from. He has no explanation for those non-material qualities in that living matter. He has to have God. But granting God, granting that first cause, he says these things develop in the conquest of life.

That is an interesting theory, until we look at the development of man. In the evolving of a man, we are told, these characteristics came to pass because of his fight for survival. The fittest survived, the others died. So that is where these qualities came from that evolved in a man.

I want to ask a simple question, and many of us do. In that evolving of a man, as he struggled for life and developed those qualities that fitted him for this life, just what part did the love of music play in that struggle for survival? What part did the love of art play in his struggle for survival? What part did the love of beauty play in that struggle for survival?

When a man looks at a sunset and sees God's colors; when a man looks at the firmament and sees the handiwork of God; when a man hears a beautiful old song and his heart responds like a chord that has been plucked, what did these things do to help him survive?

These qualities came from God! In the image of God created He him!

God loves His beautiful sunsets; He paints them with the colors of His brush. God loves His star-spangled firmament and He gave that love to the man He made. God loves the music of the spheres and the singing of the angels in Glory. Does it not say in the psalm, "Thou hast made him but a little lower than the angels and hast crowned him with glory and honor"?

These gifts of his mind, these gifts of his soul, these gifts of his heart and of his life, are not physical properties. They are non-material and non-spatial and non-metrical and non-measurable. They came from the image and the likeness of almighty God who made man and sent him forth with all the faculties with which he is now endowed.

THE STORY TOLD BY EMBRYOLOGY

CHAPTER 3

THE STORY TOLD BY EMBRYOLOGY

And God said, Let us make man in our image, after our
likeness (Gen. 1:26).

NOT ONLY IN certain academic circles, but also in certain ecclesiastical circles, the evolutionary hypothesis of
the creation of man has been accepted.

For example, I read of a great ecclesiastic who said:
"Since 1910, I have worked my way through to a rec-
ognition of the theory of evolution. Its application to
man I have during these almost 30 years come to know
as possible, as probable, as certain." This is a great divine
of the church who says that after studying thirty years
he has come to the conclusion that evolution in the development and creation of the man is a certain fact.

As I speak from this text, I am not speaking simply as
an ecclesiastic, though I do say that the theory of evolution, if it is accepted, has tremendous, immeasurable re-
percussions for the Christian faith and those repercus-
sions are tragic in the extreme. If something evolved out
of nothing, and if out of that something that evolved
out of nothing there evolved a little piece of life, an
amoeba, and if out of that amoeba there evolved a
larva, and out of that larva there evolved a fish, and
out of the fish there evolved an amphibian, and out of
the amphibian there evolved a reptile, and out of that
reptile there evolved a bird, and out of that bird there
evolved a mammal, and out of that mammal there evolved
a man, if from the beginning of emptiness and void and

nothingness until the man that is you emerges, if it is done by evolution, then there is no place for God, none at all, and you live in a material and a mechanical world.

Not only do I say that it has a repercussion in religion that is tragic, because it takes God out of life and out of the world, but I also say that it repudiates the redemptive work of Christ. If the truth of evolution is established, if the fact of it can be demonstrated, just give us more time and we will evolve into celestial and immortal archangels.

No Need for Salvation

According to the redemptive work of Christ, man was created perfect but he fell in sin and Christ was promised to restore the man to his original perfection. That redemptive work of Christ is experienced in the heart of His Christian people today. But if evolution is correct, then all of that is nothing. The Bible itself is not a revelation of God, nor is Christ the Son of God, but the Bible itself is a product of the evolutionary upreach of man seeking to find something higher and better. Just give us time and we will finally evolve into all of those wonderful and holy characteristics toward which our human hearts do faithfully long.

Can we not read? Can we not see? Can we not look? Is there anything a scientist writes that we cannot read? Is there anything he sees that we cannot see? Is there anything he says that we cannot understand? So we can see and we can look and we can read for ourselves. And this is the burden of these messages: That having looked, and having read, and having seen, there is not in science any fact to demonstrate or to prove the hypothesis of the evolutionary emergence of the man.

In the last chapter we dwelt on the fact that the *facts* of biology, not the theories nor the hypotheses, repudiate the theories and the hypotheses of evolution. In this address we are concerned with the facts of embryology. The facts of embryology rebuke, repudiate and disprove the theories of evolution.

All of life is built up of living units called cells. As a brick wall is built up of units called bricks, so all of life is made up of created units called cells. That little unit may be a complete life in itself, as a paramecium, and all of the vital functions of life are carried on in that one cell.

Or, the animal may be a metazoan. It may be made of millions and trillions of cells. In an ordinary human body there are about three hundred trillion cells, organized into that amazing complex of separate, functioning organs that make up the one great body.

In a living cell, such as a paramecium, there are three properties that are easily recognizable and observable. One is this: It has the power of spontaneous motion. In the case of an amoeba, it can stick out from itself a pseudopod, a false foot, then it can pour itself into that pseudopod, and it has moved just that much. It has the power of spontaneous motion. It can move. Again, it has the power of assimilation. Place that bit of protoplasm called an amoeba into an environment where it can assimilate food, and it will grow in size and live and carry on all of the functions of a living creature.

Then the third property in that bit of protoplasm of life is this: It has the power of reproduction. The miracle of mitosis will happen before your very eyes. That little amoeba that is one will divide and become two. And the two daughter cells will be exactly like the parent cell.

THE MIRACLE OF MITOSIS

I suppose that there is nothing more astoundingly wonderful or more miraculously marvelous in all of this world than the miracle of mitosis, cell division.

We do not have to go back into the dim ages of the past to wonder at the miraculously creative hand of God.

It is all around us; we can observe it today. Just as God wrought that miracle of creation in the beginning, we can look upon the miracle of creation this very moment, this very hour, this very day.

The miracle of mitosis begins with a living cell, the parent cell made like this: On the outside is the cell wall, and on the inside is what is called protoplasm, the living matter, made up of two parts, the cytoplasm, and the nucleus. On the inside of that nucleus are tiny granules called chromatin. That word means color and is used because the granules of the nucleus can be easily dyed or stained, so when one mounts it on a slide and looks at it under a microscope it will be clearly seen.

Now we are going to watch the cell divide, a miracle and wonder of God. First, all of the granules in the nucleus form themselves into one continuous thread, and that thread of chromatin breaks up into little rods that are called chromosomes. On either side of the cell there appear spindles, and those rods of chromosomes are drawn halfway between the spindle on this side and halfway between the spindle on that side. Each one of those chromosomes splits lengthwise, half of it drawn to one spindle, half to the other. The cell wall then closes between and there are two complete cells.

That is the miracle of mitosis. What makes it work? Who does that? Who speaks to that little cell? Who teaches it what to do?

In every species the number of chromosomes in every cell is exactly the same. There is no exception. In every cell in the body of a man there are forty-eight chromosomes. Each cell in an ox has thirty-eight chromosomes. Each cell in each lily has twenty-four chromosomes. Each cell in each fly has twelve chromosomes. There are little insects that have just two chromosomes. So all through the species, every species has its own number of chromosomes which never varies.

Now I have said that there is the full number of chromosomes in every cell of the body. There is just one exception which is this: In the reproductive cell, (in those species that reproduce by sexual attraction) the chromosomes are cut in half.

There are two kinds of cells in a man's body. There are the somatic cells, the body building cells that build the structure of anatomy. But there are also on the inside of the body of man generative cells, reproductive cells, called sperm or spermatozoa. In woman they are called ova. In man the cells of the body have forty-eight chromosomes. But in the reproductive cells there are exactly twenty-four chromosomes. In the female every cell in her body has forty-eight chromosomes. But the ovum of the woman has exactly twenty-four chromosomes. So when the two come together, the spermatozoon and the ovum, the number of the chromosomes is again complete, forty-eight. There is no exception to that — that is the iron law of the almighty God. It is the miracle of reproduction, of mitosis.

MENDEL'S LAW OF HEREDITY

There is a law of God that controls all of what we call heredity. An Austrian monk named Mendel did a wonderful work in discovering the laws of heredity, called Mendel's Law of Heredity. The work he had done was buried in the monastery with the flowers he had observed. Had that work been known to Charles Darwin the whole course of the idea and theory of evolution would have been altogether different. But Darwin did not know Mendel's Law of Heredity, and it only came to light as a rediscovery after the furious war over Charles Darwin.

Mendel's Law of Heredity is one of the great laws of God that we have discovered. It is this: the offspring inherit and produce and exhibit the characteristics of the parents according to dominant and recessive characteristics. For example, brown is dominant over blue. If there was a father who was pure brown eyed and a mother who was pure blue eyed, all of their children in the first generation would be brown-eyed, following generations differing according to a set pattern.

Mendel's Law of Heredity does two things: It makes possible the breeding of great varieties in a species. For example, one can breed speed into horses. One can have all kinds of flowers by breeding different kinds. One can have all kinds of dogs by breeding different strains of dogs. In the sperm of the male is all the ancestry of the male, and in the ovum of the female is all the ancestry of the female. So when they are brought together there are infinite possibilities of varieties. If you wanted to breed speed in a horse, you pick those varieties and breed them up. If you want to breed the heavy wool on the back of a sheep you take those strains and breed them up. If you want to add more grains on an ear of corn you have infinite opportunity by Mendel's Law to breed up these strains.

There is another fact, according to Mendel's Law, and it is this: Whatever is done to change that variety has to be done to those genes and chromosomes. It can never be done by inherited characteristics. For an offspring to change the parent has to change. The parent is the only one who can give life to an ovum or a sperm.

An embryo can never produce another embryo. It produces another parent. An egg can never produce another egg. It produces a parent which in turn produces another egg. Acquired characteristics are never inherited. You can take a dog and cut off his tail, but when that puppy has puppies they will have tails. And you can cut those tails off and cut those tails off for a hundred thousand generations and the puppies that are born will still have tails. You cannot take off or add to by an acquired characteristic. It has to be done in the gene. It has to be done in the chromosome. It has to be done in the nucleus of the ovum or of the sperm.

The only thing that can give life to an ovum or a sperm is a mature parent. So we have an endless cycle that is locked by almighty God. God said each after its kind. And the earth gave birth to all of these different kinds of animals and beasts and cattle and creeping things, each after his kind, according to the law of almighty God. Each gives birth to progeny after its kind.

THE DEVELOPING EMBRYO

So we come to the embryo, one of the most marvelous workmanships of God. When the egg is fertilized by the spermatozoon, immediately the miracle of mitosis begins to form. After awhile there comes a tube-like structure that has three layers of cells, the ectoderm, the mesoderm and the endoderm, and out of those three layers of cells that make up that tube-like creature, all of the organs of the body develop. There is a design, a hand of God that works in the multiplication of those cells. Each one of those cells, directed by an unseen hand, finally develops into the glorious organs of the body.

That original cell is not nerve cell, it is not blood cell, it is not bone cell, it is not muscle cell, it is just that seed, just that original cell, and the hand of God finally brings it into this marvelous thing that you see living about you.

What a wonderful thing! All the cells in the body differ greatly. There will be cells of the brain, and cells of the lung, and cells of the stomach, and cells of the bone, but all of those cells will have the same number of chromosomes in them, and every cell in the human body will be a human cell. Every cell in a chicken will be a chicken cell. Every cell in a rabbit will be a rabbit cell, and every cell in every creature God has made will be according to that cell. The Lord wrote that in His Book, in I Corinthians, the fifteenth chapter and thirty-ninth verse. To paraphrase, Paul says: "All protoplasm is not the same protoplasm, but there is one kind of protoplasm of men, and another protoplasm of beasts, and another of fishes, and another of birds." The protoplasm in all these species is different. Give any tissue to a scientist and he can immediately identify whether it belongs to a man, to a beast, to a fowl or to some other kind of creature.

Now may we consider the evolutionary hypothesis which is called the recapitulation theory. The recapitulation theory of the evolutionist is this: That in the development of the human embryo it relives all of the stages of its evolutionary ancestry.

You see, the evolutionist says we started from a protozoon, a little amoeba, then we came up through a worm, then through a fish, and an amphibian, a reptile, fowl, mammal and finally a man. So the recapitulation theory of the evolutionist is that the human embryo, as it develops into a human being, exhibits all of that ancestry of the past. It first is a protozoon. Then it is a fish and lives in an aqueous environment. Then it has a tail like a dog. Then it is a mammal fetus like the fetus of an ape, and then finally it emerges a man. The recapitulation theory of the evolutionist is that the story of the development of the human embryo recapitulates or summarizes all of that evolutionary past. That is the sheerest nonsense, that is the sheerest insanity that you will ever find among so-called scientific facts.

For example, let us take the first, that the human embryo begins as a protozoon, a little amoeba. I do not think there is any creditable scientist in this world who would ever mix up, or be unable to distinguish between, a little amoeba and the egg that turns into a man. He just would not do it. Were we able to get on the inside of that protozoon and walk around and look at it, and were we able to get on the inside of the egg that finally becomes a man, we would find the difference between them as much as between a locomotive and a pipe organ. Because both of them are small, and because both of them are unicellular means nothing at all. They are vastly different in every one of their parts. The protozoon is a complete animal. It can eat, it can assimilate, it can reproduce, it lives a whole life, but the egg is the seed of a man, and the genes and the chromosomes and the whole outreach of its life are altogether different.

The second idea, that the embryo lives like a fish and has gills, is ridiculous when we look at it. The embryo is alive on the inside of an amniotic sack filled with amniotic fluid. The sack around an embryo is called an amnion. It is cushioned on every side by the amniotic fluid. They say the embryo is an aqueous creature and that it lives in water like a fish, but there is no resemblance between that embryo and a fish. A fish lives in water and breathes free oxygen from the water. A fetus does not breathe at all. The oxygen comes into its life stream from the blood of the mother, but it does not breathe at all, and there is no free oxygen in that amniotic fluid, none at all.

Then we are told that at a certain stage the embryo has gills like a fish. Here is what happens: As that embryo begins to form, at the early stages it develops arches, little bony ridges like the ridges that support the gills of a fish. So some evolutionists look at those ridges and say, "Look, these are the gills of a fish." The arches of the fish have to do with respiration, they have to do with breathing. But the fetus does not breathe. It has no cause for breathing at all, but it does have a cause to live, to eat, to be nourished, without which nourishment it would die.

When the embryo is just a tiny thing, that amniotic fluid is almost altogether pure food, fats and carbohydrates and proteins. Later it changes in character and the fluid could not be used for food but at that stage all of the fluid around the embryo is made up of pure food. Those little arches the scientists look at and say are gills of a fish, actually absorb that food; that is their purpose. Then later when the embryo begins to get its food from the mother's blood, there is no need for those pharyngeal arches and they disappear. But they are in no wise like the gills of a fish, nor are they used or built to serve the purpose served by the arches that support the gills of a fish. There is no resemblance whatsoever. They are for altogether different purposes.

We are also told that at a certain time the embryo has a tail like a dog. When the embryo is about the size of a lima bean there is a little unusual activity in the posterior region. But give that little tail time to develop and it develops into legs. The structures of tails and legs are altogether different. Nor is there anywhere in anatomy or in embryology or in the development of life that a tail develops into a leg. It just does not. And there is no resemblance in them at all.

Then last, we are told that the fetus of a man is like that of a mammal, like that of an ape, and when an ape embryo and a man embryo are compared, they look alike. Therefore, they must have come from the same thing. I cannot understand the reasoning of men when they say things like that. There are many poisons that look exactly like sugar and like salt, but that does not make them all alike. One is a poison and one is sugar and one is salt.

The reason things look alike is that God made them on the same pattern. In this world all of us have to breathe alike. All of us have to eat alike, and the same matchless hand of God that made us made the animal and all of this world. Consider the wheel. There will be a wheel on a wheelbarrow, a wheel on an automobile, a wheel on a great locomotive. They are all wheels. They are the same type, because they show a common efficiency in movement. So it is with God's workmanship. When you look at an object of creation there are many objects that are similar to it. But they are similar only on the basis that we live in the same world and the great creative hand of God did all of it. But as for its being exactly alike, similarity has nothing to do with it. The embryo of the man will be one thing; the embryo of an ape will be another thing; the embryo of a monkey will be another thing, and if you don't believe it, just give them time to develop so your eyes can see the vast difference between the two.

The facts of embryology repudiate the theories of evolution. God said, "Let us create man in our image, in our likeness, and in the image of God created he him." And the miracle that happened in the Garden of Eden is the same miracle that happens today as we look upon it with our very eyes — God's creation of the man in His own image and in His own likeness.

WE VISIT THE MUSEUM

CHAPTER 4

WE VISIT THE MUSEUM

IN THE FIRST chapter of Genesis, the twenty-fourth and twenty-fifth verses, God's Word says,

> And God said, Let the earth bring forth the living creature after his kind, cattle, and creeping thing, and beast of the earth after his kind: and it was so. And God made the beast of the earth after his kind, and cattle after their kind, and every thing that creepeth upon the earth after his kind: And God saw that it was good.

No one could read this Scripture without noticing the repetition of a certain thing that God's Word says, that God made every living creature "after his kind," cattle, creeping thing, beast of the earth. Then it is repeated, "And God made the beast of the earth after his kind, cattle after their kind, everything that creepeth upon the earth after his kind." The Bible gives a conclusive and definite statement about how God created these life forms. Each one He created in a family group after his kind, and these family units called species are never broken. They are unbreakable units in the creative act of God.

We have been speaking along the lines of biology and embryology, and now we come to the witness of paleontology or fossilology — that is, what is the record of the earth, the geological ages of this earth? What has God written in the rocks? Does what God writes in the rocks

corroborate what God writes in the Book or are they two
different things? The evolutionist says that what is written
in the Bible and what is written in the rocks are contradictory. If that is true, then what is written in the Bible is
untrue. If we can read contradiction in the rocks to what
God has written in the Word, then I am willing to give
up the Word. If it can be an established fact that what
I see written in the geological formations of the world
contradicts what I read in the Bible, I am willing to give
up the Bible. But the thesis of this pastor is that what
God has written in His rocks is the same as what God has
written in His Book. And we can examine the evidence
ourselves. We can read the Bible and we can see the
rocks. So, that is what we're going to do in this and the
following address.

We are going to the museum and look at some of the
fossils that have been aggregated and arranged to support the theory of evolution.

A few months ago I was traveling across this continent
by plane, and as I sat by the side of a young man, I
opened a magazine, and on the inside there happened to
be an article on the creation of the world and the creation of life, or as the article was presenting it, on the evolution of the world and the evolution of the forms of life.
As I began to look at it, I noticed the young fellow next
to me was interested and I began to talk to him about it.
I found that he was a young professor in the University
of California at Los Angeles, so we began to talk about
evolution, and he was amazed, he was astounded, to learn
that I believed in the Bible and that I believed those old
"legends and myths and fictional presentations" that are
found in the Book of Genesis. So a discussion was precipitated between us. As we went on the professor floored
me with this word. He said: "Evolution is a demonstrable fact and you can see it for yourself. I have seen
it. In a certain museum you can see from fossil life how

the horse has developed from a four-toed cat to the great draft Clydesdale of modern times."

"Well," I said, "You're sure of that?"

He said, "I am sure of it. I have seen it for myself."

I said, "Well, if that's so, I'm just lost. I'm wrong. Everything I think and believe just isn't so, it isn't true."

It was one of the good fortunes of my life that recently being on the Pacific coast, I made my way to that museum and visited the fossils of which that young professor spoke. So, you and I are going to visit that museum.

HALLS OF EVOLVING LIFE

First, when I walked in the door, I saw on the right a long poster entitled, "The Histomat of Evolution," and then the sub-title. "Ten Thousand Million Years" (that would be ten billion years) "Ten Thousand Million Years of Evolution on a Single Page"! So I looked at the page, and on the inside read, "Line of Descent from Amoeba to Man." From the amoeba we developed into unsegmented worms; then we developed into sea squirts; then we developed into vertebrates; then primitive sharks; then amphibians; then reptiles; then mammals, then monkeys; then apes; then the Piltdown Man — I especially noticed him (later we are going into the hoaxes of anthropology); and finally, we developed into man. The foreword stated:

> The subject of evolution has been considered as being opposed to religious principles. It is becoming increasingly evident, however, that a wider dissemination of the scientific data of biological evolution will have only one result — the building of a new and a greater faith in life. It brings realization of an upward trend in bodily function and mental powers. Is not this the best possible guarantee of further evolution toward something higher and better?

Do you see? In the foreword of that Histomat of Evolution the writer says that this does not contravene religious principles but it builds a new and greater faith in life. But it doesn't build it in God. It is a repudiation of God. It leaves God out. It empties the universe of God. Men for awhile will follow religious ceremonies that have been emptied of their meaning, but not for long. It is not long after the religious content has been emptied of its faith and of its pertinency and of its revelation and of its truth, it is not long until thinking men abandon those religious forms. And that happens to any man's soul when he embraces atheistic, materialistic evolution! He may be religious for a while. His children may have a half-way form of religion, but after awhile they give it up altogether. Why? Because it has no meaning, it has no pertinency. If there is no God, and if God is not in this world, and if He did not make it and if He does not control it, and if there is not a God to whom someday we shall give an account, why bother with the supposed fictional fact of God? The writer of the Histomat of Evolution said in essence, "Give us time, just give us days, give us hours, give us a hundred million years, and we will all develop into archangels." But God says an altogether different thing about humanity. God says we were created perfect and fell into sin, and from that fall we cannot redeem ourselves. Then comes the unfolding of the great plan of the ages in the redemptive sacrifice of the Lord Jesus Christ. But let's go on into the museum.

On the inside of that great, world-famous museum is a hall entitled, "The Hall of Evolving Life." Underneath this caption these words are inscribed: "This hall is designed to demonstrate the capacity of change inherent in all life, and that change goes hand in hand with the gradual evolution of life forms throughout the ages." What a wonderful prospect! We are now entering a great museum, one of the great halls in that museum called the Hall of Evolving Life, and we are going inside of that wonderful, scientific hall in order to see unveiled before us the forms of evolving life. We are going to have a final answer to this question about how the many, many life forms about us came into being. So we enter the hall. And what do I see? First, there is a skull of a New World monkey. Then by the side of that there is a skull of an Old World monkey. Then by that there is the skull of an ape; and by the side of that is the skull of a man. The skulls of the monkeys look like monkey skulls to me — animal skulls. The skull of a man looks like a man's skull.

The second exhibit is this: There is the exhibit of the skeleton of a man. By that is the exhibit of the skeleton of a chimpanzee. The skeleton of a man looks like the skeleton of a man to me, and the skeleton of the chimpanzee looks like the skeleton of a chimpanzee to me. In the next exhibit the leg bones of eight or nine mammals are shown.

All this is supposed to be a demonstration of the evolution of life. I could not believe that men who are supposed to be trained and supposed to be scientists propose to demonstrate such a far-reaching doctrine as the evolutionary hypothesis by just putting behind those glass windows these several skeletons that can be found almost anywhere in the earth. It is the same as if you took the houses that you see in this world, and having noticed they all have floors, they all have ceilings, they all have walls, they all have windows, they all have doors, you classified and arranged them according to an ascending scale. Here you have a little dog house. There you have a big dog house. Over there you have a shanty, a shack. Then you have a cottage, then you have a little house, then you have a big house, then you have a mansion, then you have a castle. And when you get them all arranged you say, "See, this castle evolved out of that little dog house." The man who objects will say, "But you're talking about

inanimate things and inanimate things don't evolve."
When I say that little dog houses do not evolve into
castles and you say that is because they are inanimate
objects, that is not half as ridiculous and preposterous as
when the evolutionist says that dead, inanimate matter
evolved into all these forms. But that is what the evolutionist would have me to believe when he says that all of
these living organisms we see today evolved out of dead,
inert matter, spontaneously of its own inherent chemical
powers.

Why, this exhibit of bones proves not a thing in the
world. If a man is looking for something it does prove,
it is this: That the infinite and all-wise God, when He
made all of the different forms of life, gave to all of
those forms the finest construction that He could devise.
The finest construction of a bone is the bone that you
see. The finest construction of muscles are the muscles
that you see. The finest construction of nerves are the
nerves that you see. So God did not change one original
being into different species, but He gave the best to each
one. All of us have to eat, and all of us live in the same
world, and all of us breathe the same air. Therefore, the
structural forms will be much alike, the bones of an ape,
the nerves of an ape, the muscles of an ape; the bones of
a man, the muscles of a man, the nerves of a man.
God chose the best form and He gave it to the animals
that He created and He gave it to the man that He made.
And that is all that those structural likenesses indicate.
But as for one evolving out of the other, there is no sem-
blance of proof in it at all.

THE ASCENT OF EQUUS

Now, let us go to the main exhibit. This is the thing
that I had been looking forward to for a long, long time.
There it was on the mezzanine entitled "The Ascent of
Equus," the ascent of the horse, the evolution of the horse.

The caption underneath the headline was, "The Ascent of Equus — beginning with Eohippus." The Greek word for horse is *hippos*. So the Eohippus would be "dawn-horse," the beginning horse. Beginning with Eohippus, this exhibit traces the development of the horse through forty-five million years of natural evolution and a few hundred years of domestication. We are now going to see unfolded before our eyes forty-five million years of natural evolution of the horse. Why, my fingers tingled, my eyes dilated, my mind quickened, everything about me sprang up. What a great exhibit am I going to see! Then, this is what I saw. There were five exhibits of skeletons of horses. Number one: "Pliocene Horse Plesippus Shochonenis. Early one-toed horse of two million years ago. From upper Pliocene Hagerman Beds, Idaho." I looked at the skeleton and it was the skeleton of a horse. Just an ordinary horse. Just a horse. I looked at the sign and read it again, "Early One-Toed Horse of Two Million Years Ago." Well, the "one-toe" was just his hoof, like any horse's hoof.

The second skeleton is a Pleistocene Horse, Equus Occidentalis. On our side. Not Orientalis — Occidentalis, a western horse. "Western Horse of California Fifty Thousand Years Ago. Extinct before historic times, from Rancho LaBrea (that's the Spanish word for tar, asphalt) Pleistocene Asphalt Deposits." I looked at that horse and he had one toe, too, just like the other horse, but it never mentioned that, and the second skeleton looked exactly like the first one, just a little larger and one million nine hundred fifty thousand years later.

The third exhibit was a domestic horse, labeled such. The fourth exhibit was an Arabian horse, and the fifth and last exhibit was the skeleton of a draft horse. I looked at it and I said: "Surely there's something more around here than that! There's bound to be something more than this because they're going to demonstrate to me fifty million years of the ascent of equus and all I have here are just five skeletons of horses." So I looked around and I found it. By the mezzanine rail there was a little glass case with the sign: "Earliest American Horse. Plaster Replica of Eohippus Borealis." Borealis refers to the north, and Eohippus, the dawn-horse. The northern dawn-horse. The caption read: "Eohippus Borealis. Earliest known ancestor of the modern horse. Lived in North America during the Lower Eocene fifty million years ago. The remains are fragmentary. Only rarely do we find fossil material complete enough to permit construction of a mounted skeleton." In other words, guess work. The card went on to say that the head of that animal did not belong to the body but was just put with the body in order to display it there in the case. The sign continued: "Striking Difference. Tiny size. Thirteen Inches High. Long Body with Arched Back. Four Functional Digits on Front Feet, Three Functional Digits on Hind Feet. Teeth and Feet Indicate a Browsing (that is, ate tender leaves and bark) Rather than a Grazing Animal." So, we have it there in the little glass case, a little cat-like animal with four toes on its front feet and three toes on its hind feet.

That horse is the classic demonstration of the evolutionist to show the facts supposedly supporting his hypothesis. When you ask an evolutionist, "Where can you demonstrate with a fossil any species that developed and evolved?" he will point to the prize exhibit, the horse. If the extravagant reproductions they make of that horse, and all those paintings by which they present him are true, that the great draft animal we know today evolved from what looks more like a civet cat than anything else, I will admit that evolutionists have pretty well beyond question, demonstrated their hypothetical theory.

But there are several things to be said about the horse. I read on the case that that little Eocene animal lived fifty million years ago, and the next demonstration was of the

Pleistocene animal two million years ago. Evolutionists
have to account for forty-eight million years of time, and in
that forty-eight million years of time they must find the
missing links between that little civet cat and the horse
as we know it today. Where are those missing links? That
is why I went to the museum. I was eager to see those
missing links. They are not there.

The second fact is this: The arrangement of the demonstration is purely arbitrary. From what I read, in the
American Museum of Natural History in New York City
there are twelve exhibits, whereas in this great museum
on the west coast there are just six. But the second observation I make about it is this: The arrangement of those
exhibits is altogether arbitrary. They pick out an animal
and they say, this animal evolved into that animal. That
is not so. This animal belongs to a species of its own,
and this next animal belongs to a species of its own, and
this animal belongs to a species of its own. All of these
species are unbreakable units in themselves. They did not
evolve from one to the other.

The third fact is the main point. In the same fossil
stratum where one finds that little animal called Eohippus
in the Eocene Age, in that same stratum can be found a
real horse, an actual horse, a horse like the modern horse.
Why doesn't the evolutionist put that in his exhibit?
Because a horse cannot evolve out of a horse; he is a horse
already. Therefore, he cannot be put in the display. At
the same time the prehistoric camel lived, and at the same
time the saber-tooth tiger lived, and at the same time
those great mammals lived, and at the same time those
great elephants lived — at that same time the horse lived.
And one can find the fossil skeleton of the horse in the
same stratum in which he finds all the rest of them. And
yet they say this little animal evolved into the horse. But
we already have a horse! He is already there, side by side

in the same forest, and in the same pasture, and in the same world, and at the same time.

My last avowal is this: The evolutionist is deceived by his own principles of arrangement. Today as I walk around, as I look, I see for children to ride, a little Shetland pony. And then, there are tremendous Clydesdale horses. But, do you know, between the little Shetland pony and the great draft Clydesdale there are intermediate forms all the way through. There is the zebra, the western broom-tailed bronco, the saddle horse, the Arabian racer, the thoroughbred racer, the Percheron and then the great Clydesdale. They are all there in the same family.

Now, let us suppose they all died, and they are all buried in mud, and the mud becomes fossil, and fifty million years from now men digging down there find those fossil skeletons. Oh, what a case for evolution. Look here — look there — the little Shetland pony. Look there. Ah, it is demonstrated. They all evolved from those little animals to these big animals. Not so. *They were all contemporary.* That is my point.

The amoeba is the contemporary of the man. The paramecium is the contemporary of the man. The worm is the contemporary of the man. The amphibian is the contemporary of the man and the fish. The reptile and the fowl, the beasts of the field, all of them are the contemporaries of the man. And when they appeared, each species appeared by the creative act of God suddenly. They appeared complete and whole just like God made them, and just as we read the account in the Bible.

THE RECORD OF THE ROCKS

CHAPTER 5

THE RECORD OF THE ROCKS

IN THE FIRST chapter of Genesis, the twenty-sixth and twenty-seventh verses we read:

> And God said, Let us make man in our image, after our likeness. . . . So God created man in his own image, in the image of God created he him; male and female created he them.

The Scriptures say of this creation that God created

> . . . the moving creature that hath life, and fowl that may fly above the earth in the open firmament of heaven . . . and every living creature that moveth (in the waters), after their kind . . . and every winged fowl after his kind. And God said, Let the earth bring forth the living creature after his kind, cattle, and creeping thing, and beast of the earth after his kind. And God made the beast of the earth after his kind, and cattle after their kind, and every thing that creepeth upon the earth after his kind: and God saw that was good (Gen. 1:20-22).

The creation of all of life and its forms that we see in this world, the Scriptures say, God did according to a pattern. And that pattern is fixed, God says. It is locked. It is unbreakable. God created all of these forms of life, the Scriptures say, after their kind. He did it by family units. (He did it by species.)

We are going now to the record of the rocks and we are going to see if what God has written in His Book is the same thing God has written in His rocks.

The study of paleontology or fossilology is a study of life of the geological ages of the long ago. It differs from botany and zoology and biology in that the life it observes, the individuals it studies, are in fossil form — they lived long ago.

The Ages of Geology

The study of geology is the study of the geological ages of the earth. It is a study of the rocks. The geologist divides the supposed history of this earth into six enormous periods. And in order for us to enter this brief study of fossilology, we want to acquaint ourselves with these terms that the paleontologist will often use — these geological ages and periods of our earth.

A great division of time is called an era. The era is divided into periods. The first geological age is called Azoic. The Greek word for life is *zoe,* so these syllables, zoic, refer to life. The azoic era was in the dim and undated past before there was any such thing as life — azoic.

The second era is called Archeozoic. The Greek word for ancient is *archaois;* the Greek word for beginning is *arche,* so archeozoic is back in the beginning. That age is dated about one billion years ago.

The third geological era is called Proterozoic. The Greek word for before, or earlier, is *proteros.* The Proterozoic is the geological age six hundred and fifty million years ago.

The fourth geological age is Paleozoic. *Palaios* means old and ancient. Paleozoic is the era of one hundred million years ago and is divided into several periods, some of which are common in the books we read in the study of paleontological subjects. These are some of the periods in the Paleozoic Age: the Cambrian, the Silurian, the Carboniferous and the Permian. All of these are periods in the Paleozoic Age.

The fifth geological era is called Mesozoic. *Mesos* is the Greek word for middle. So Mesozoic is the geological age, they say, seventy million years ago. It is divided into the Triassic, the Jurassic and the Cretaceous periods. The Latin word for chalk is *creta,* and from the chalk formations in that age we have the name Cretaceous. Then the last geological age is Cenozoic. The Greek word for recent, new, is *kainos,* and from it comes the word, Cenozoic. The Cenozoic Age, the recent age, begins at fifty million years ago. It is divided into periods, the names of which you will often come across in geology or paleontology. One is Eocene. The Greek word for dawn is *eos,* and of course *kainos,* recent, so the Eocene is the recent dawn age. The *Miocene: meion* means less, so the Miocene Age. Then the Pliocene: *pleion* means more, greater — the Pliocene Age. The next period is the Pleistocene: *pleistos* means most, greatest. And then finally we come to the human age.

The method by which geologists know to date those ages is this: In any lake, or in any ocean, there will be sediments—sand and gravel and mud—that settle to the bottom of the waters. During the ages, the sediment — sand and gravel and mud—in many instances turns into solid rock. In the convulsions of the earth in the ages past, great bodies of dry land that we now see were once the bottom of these bodies of water. When the bottoms of some of those oceans and some of those great lakes were pushed up and made into mountains and high plateaus, this made it possible for us to read the record of the history of the earth from the layers that were desposited in the bottom of the ocean or of the lake.

For example, if you ever go to Grand Canyon, which is a geologist's paradise, you will see differing layers all the way from the top, thousands of feet above, clear down to the basalt through which the Colorado River is now cutting its way. The bottom part is the original earth. That above it has been deposited in separate layers through the geological ages.

Now, with this brief background of the layers in which

we are going to look for life, let us begin the study of fossils.

THE FORMATION OF FOSSILS

A <u>fossil</u> is a plant or an animal that lived long, long ago. We find its traces, the record of its life, in fossil remains.

There are many, many kinds of fossils. One example is this: A leaf grew in one of those geological ages and fell into soft, limy mud, and was covered with that mud. The leaf gradually decayed, but as it decayed it was replaced with limy mud. In the geological ages that followed, the mud turned to solid rock. When one breaks the rock there is the perfect cast of the leaf — the raised figure of the leaf on the smooth surface of the split stone. That is a fossil.

In one of those geological ages, an animal walked over soft mud. Sediments were washed into the footprints so gently that the footprints were not disturbed. In the ages that passed the layer of mud turned into solid rock, and there, imprinted forever in stone, are the footprints of an ancient animal. That is a fossil.

Another kind of fossil is a petrified bone. There sank to the bottom of the waters the bones of animals, and those bones were covered over with slime and mud. And in the ages that passed, the water gradually dissolved, particle by particle, the material of the bone, and deposited in its place precipitate of chalk or of some other matter. Finally, the entire bone was dissolved, but in its place there is an exact replica of that bone in solid stone. That is a fossil.

Another kind of fossil results when a substance has captured the body of an animal and has preserved it without decaying. For example, in the Carboniferous Age, which is dated something like one hundred million years ago, the conifers, the coniferous tree, exuded gum and resin which fell on the ground and ran down the sides of the trunks of the trees. Little insects and ants would get caught in that resin. The resin was buried in the ground, and in the years and the ages past, the resin turned into what we call amber. In some of that amber we can see perfectly preserved the entire bodies of the little ants or the insects that were trapped therein. That is a fossil.

Another kind of a fossil is an animal trapped in the glacial ice. After the passing of ages and ages one can find in the glacial ice the entire body of the animal that lived so long ago. That is a fossil.

Another example of fossils is to be found in the La Brea tar pits in southern California. After a heavy rain the pools were covered in water, and great animals going down to drink, unaware of the terrible tar pools beneath the surface of the water, were caught therein. They became death traps for great mastodons and dinosaurs and giant sloths. There they are in fossil form, as they have been for millions of years past.

In this world, for a man to look at, there are uncounted billions and billions and billions of fossils. I read of one ledge in California that is exposed about six hundred feet deep and about half a mile long, and it is estimated that in that one ledge alone there are more than ten billion fossils, and there is no telling how many others there are because we do not know how deep into the mountain the ledge extends. So fossil life is everywhere; it is multitudinous, and any man who wishes to study it can find it without end.

The theory of evolution is this: All of the forms of life that we now see came from one primordial protozoon. There was a common ancestor in the beginning — whenever that was, whenever it started — there was a common one-celled ancestor from which all of the forms of life have now developed. There was a little amoeba-like bit of protoplasm that felt the first faint stirrings of ambition, and it started out on that long, arduous journey that millions

and millions of years later finally fruited in the crowning
animal which calls himself *homo sapiens.* That is the
theory of evolution.

Along the way as that amoeba-like protoplasm developed into the man that we see today, along the
way there incidentally developed about one hundred
twenty-five million different species. That was just inci-
dental as the little amoeba-like bit of protoplasm began
to evolve into this man who calls himself *homo sapiens.*
Now, you would expect to find in the geological record
of this earth, if that is true — if we have drifted from one
species into another, if the fish drift over into four-legged
amphibians, and if the four-legged amphibians gradually
drift over into birds, if the scales turn into feathers, and
if the feathers turn into wings, and if the snakes sprout
legs and fur — if all of these reptiles finally turn into
mammals and these marsupials turn into apes and finally
into men, you would expect to find all of that plainly,
distinctly in the great fossilological ages of the past,
wouldn't you? There we have the record of life from the
beginning, and the evolutionist says that all of these
species drifted into one another as they gradually evolved
up from the little speck of protoplasm to the man that
you see today. So, with great anticipation, with wonderful interest, we are going to turn our faces to the rocks
and see if we can find in those rocks the record of that
evolutionary story that the evolutionist says is so plainly
manifest.

What Do the Rocks Say?

What do the rocks say? The rocks say three things.
First, the record of the rocks is exactly like the record
of the Book. The record of the rocks says that life appeared suddenly. It burst into this world with teeming
complexity and diversity. The rocks say that when a
family appears it appears whole and complete and fitted
for the environment in which it was made to live. It

appears without antecedents and without previous development. For example, when the fish appears he has his fin, and he has his gills, he has his scales and he has all of the appurtenances for living in water. When the fowls appear, the birds appear with their wings, and they appear with their plumes and they appear with all of the other habiliments that go with a winged bird. And when the first armadillo appears, there he is bearing the same impenetrable armor that his progeny bear. All of these families, all of these species, when they appear, appear suddenly and just as they are, complete and furnished for life. Those that need teeth have teeth; those that need gizzards have gizzards. Everything is furnished just as God has made it. Well, isn't that a remarkable thing! There is no evidence at all that any of these forms of life that we see in those geological ages, ever developed, or that they ever evolved, from antecedents. How do you explain that?

Charles Darwin attempted a feeble explanation, and it is this: "Geology assuredly does not reveal any such finely graded organic chain; and this perhaps is the most obvious and serious objection which can be urged against the theory. The explanation lies, however, in the extreme imperfection of the geologic record." Is that not an odd thing? The record suffers from "extreme imperfection" when it comes to the point that we want to know, when it comes to bridging over these families, when it comes to demonstrating the evolving of one species from another. Darwin says the geological record suffers from "extreme imperfection." But the geological record is filled with data, multitudinous data when it comes to exhibiting the separate families and the separate species themselves. There are thousands of billions of organisms to be seen in fossil life, and all of them are in those fixed, unbreakable units that we call families or species. There is not any instance in geology or in paleontology where one species ever developed over into another. Darwin says the reason it cannot be proved lies in the "extreme imperfection" of the geological record. The truth of the matter is there is no such thing in geological time, as in modern time, where any of those species ever changed or evolved from one into the other. That is one of the tremendous blows to the evolutionary hypothesis.

Life began, so they say, in the Cambrian layer, which is dated something like a hundred million years ago. When one comes to what is called the Cambrian layer, it is filled with thousands and thousands of fossils and all of those creatures are diversified and complex. Life immediately and suddenly appears. In the pre-Cambrian layers, in the layers of the Proterozoic Era, there is no life at all, none at all. Then, come to the Cambrian layer and there life teems, it bursts suddenly into this world — without development, without evolution. So all of the families of life, when you see them in geological strata, appear suddenly and they all appear complete. The first bat is a true bat. The first whale is a true whale. The first shark is a true shark. The first anything is a true whatever family it is. And it shows no evolving at all, no gradual development from previous species. When you see it in geological record, there it is just the same as you see it today.

Why is it that the evolutionist will not admit that thing that he sees with his own eyes? Even the great evolutionist, LeComte du Nouy, well-known French scientist, in his book, *Human Destiny,* which was hailed as a brilliant contribution to the theory of evolution, admitted: "Each group, order, or family seems to be born suddenly and we hardly ever find the forms which link them to the preceding strain. When we discover them they are already completely differentiated. Not only do we find practically no transitional forms, but in general it is impossible to authentically connect a new group with an ancient one." He admits that the reptiles appear suddenly, that they cannot be linked with any of their terrestrial ancestors, and he makes the same admission regarding mammals. About birds he says, "They have all the unsatisfactory characteristics of absolute creation."

Why does LeComte du Nouy refer to absolute creation as being "unsatisfactory"? The answer is this: The evolutionist looks upon special creation as it is recorded by the hand of God in the Book of Genesis, as a thing not to be seen and a thing not to be heard and a thing not to be spoken of. He is prejudiced against the creative act of God and he looks upon it as an evil not to be admitted.

For example, Sir Arthur Keith said: "Evolution is unproved and unprovable. We believe it because the only alternative is special creation, and that is unthinkable." Professor D. M. S. Watson of the University of London said: "Evolution itself is accepted by zoologists, not because it has been observed to occur or can be proved by logically coherent evidence to be true, but because the only alternative, special creation, is clearly incredible." The evolutionist begins with an a priori judgment that there is no such thing as God's creative act, therefore anything that proves special creation is immediately cast aside and scorned and ridiculed. Everything that can be marshaled together, whether it is true or untrue, is in order to prove an unprovable theory, to demonstrate an untrue hypothesis. Anything is used in writing, drawing, imagination and plaster of Paris to pervert the simple truth of the Scriptures.

The first evidence that we see from the record of the rocks is this, that life appeared suddenly, just as the Bible states, and that when life appeared suddenly it appeared in fixed families and species just as the Bible account gives the record. First comes plant life in those geological ages. Then, second, comes animal life in those geological ages. And finally, the appearance of the man that God made — the first thing to be learned from the record of the rocks.

No Fossil Transitional Forms

The second thing we learn from the record of the rocks is this: There are no transitional forms from species to species. Recently at a meeting of the scientists of the University of California, a note was sent out that was broadcast and published in the papers saying that they were now developing the theory that evolution had stopped, regarding mankind, at least. That is a great admission, is it not? As though a blind man could not see that. Yes, evolution is stopped, they say, with regard to us now. The record of the rocks says that what we see now is the same thing we could have seen long ago.

There is no evolution now; there was no evolution then. There was no transferring from species to species then, just as there is not now. There is no evolving now, there is no changing now. We do not see cats turning into dogs, and we do not see dogs turning into cows, and we do not see cows turning into horses, and we do not see horses turning into apes, and apes into men. We do not see it now: We do not see it back there in the fossilological ages of the past. The same fixity of species seen today is the same fixity of species seen in the geological ages of the past; there is no difference. The way God runs his world today is the same way that God ran his world then.

For example, in the Cambrian layer (the first stratum of the Paleozoic Age which is dated one hundred million years ago) there were formed in this world moss agates. The rising of water from the lower parts of the earth carried variegated chalcedonies through mineral salts. When the water evaporated, those different chemicals precipitated. Sometimes the water would have in it oxide of iron or oxide of zinc or oxide of lead, and having no affinity with the chalcedony, formed beautiful exquisite patterns called moss agates. In one of the moss agates I read about, there is trapped a little mosquito. That mosquito was trapped in the moss agate, according to their reckoning, something like one hundred million years ago. And he is exactly like his fearful, pestiferous progeny today. Aren't you glad he didn't evolve! Evolution, they say, comes from the simple to the complex, from the little to the big. In a hundred million years if he had been evolving mosquitos today roaming around this earth would have been as big as eagles. Aren't you glad he is just the same?

In the Silurian Age, which, we are told, is something less than one hundred million years ago, were the coral polyps working in the bottom of the ocean, and back there were the algae. The coral of today and the little algae of today are exactly as they were one hundred million years ago; they have not changed an iota. The evolutionist is always hiding behind the fact that this cannot be observed, cannot be seen. He says the process cannot be seen because it takes millions of years for it to happen. Here are coral, here are algae, the lowly animals, that we can observe as they worked one hundred million years ago. And he is the same polyp, he is the same alga today as he was one hundred million years ago; he hasn't evolved at all.

Or, let us take the little creature of the Carboniferous Age. Caught in amber he is the same ant, he is the same insect of today, he has not evolved at all. Or take the crayfish in the Carboniferous Era; they were everywhere, and they are the same today as they were then.

There are great deposits of Eocene Age fossil life in the Pacific Coast range. It used to be a part of the Pacific Ocean, now it has been raised up seven or eight thousand feet. There one can find the great shark, there one can find the great whale, there one can find all kinds of fish, and they are the same kind that one can find in the Pacific Ocean today. And the Eocene Age is dated fifty million years ago.

There is a grasshopper glacier of the Pleistocene Era (something less than fifty million years ago), in Montana. In the glacial period, those grasshoppers going in front of the approaching cold fell by the millions and the millions into the lake. They froze there and the lake became a part of the glacier, and one can see those grasshoppers in the glacier today just as they were when they were frozen there fifty million years ago, and they are the same kind of grasshoppers we have today.

I have one other thing about the record of the rocks. The first record of the rocks was this: Life appeared suddenly, and each family when it appeared, appeared in its unbreakable unit, whole and complete. The second avowal was that there was no changing from one species to the other, but the species were fixed in geological age as it is today.

A third avowal: <u>If there is any change as you look at geology, as you look at fossilology, if there is any change it is not up, it is not evolving, it is not evolution. If there is any change, it is devolution — it is degeneration.</u> And there is no exception that we can find. For example, when I went out to the museum I saw there the fossil skeleton of an enormous elephant, the "Elephas Imperator." The biggest elephant that we have had was called Jumbo, and everyone paid to see Jumbo. Why, he is a pigmy compared to the elephants we used to have! Instead of going up, they are coming down.

If life is changing, if life is evolving, it is not going up: It is coming down. That is what the record of the rocks says. And the record of the rocks is exactly like the record of the Book!

THE HOAXES OF ANTHROPOLOGY

CHAPTER 6

THE HOAXES OF ANTHROPOLOGY

> And God said, Let us make man in our image, after our
> likeness . . . So God created man in his own image, in the
> image of God created he him; male and female created he them
> . . . And the Lord God formed man out of the dust of the
> ground, and breathed into his nostrils the breath of life; and man
> became a living soul (Gen. 1:26, 27; 2:7).

THE WITNESS of the revelation in the first chapters of
Genesis is clear and plain. God created man in the image
of God and breathed into his nostrils the breath of life,
and man became a living soul.

There is no question and no doubt about this creation,
about the structure, inward and outward, of the man,
as we read the Bible. He is differentiated from the beast.
God made the animal of the field separate and apart.
After the Lord God had created the fish of the sea and
the fowl of the air and the beast of the field, then the
Lord God created man in His own image and in his own
likeness.

That is one way of explaining all of the forms of
life that we see around us. They were created by the
Lord God. Everything we see was made by the hands
of God. Out of nothing, He created our universe. And
in that universe He created life and the forms of life that
we see, grouped by family units. God created them so,
and God fastened those family units in unbreakable links.
Each one of the families, each one of the species, is a unit
in itself. Each after his own kind. God made it that way.

In those created units is the family of man. God made

him separate and apart. God created him as such. The
Bible says that God created him perfect. All of his faculties — intellectual, physical, spiritual — all of his faculties
were given to him in the day that God created him.

From that perfect and exalted estate, man fell because
of sin. Some of the children of Adam went down and
down until we see their degradation in the squalor of the
lowest savage.

But God had pity upon the children of Adam, who
thus fell into sin and iniquity, and who thus degraded
their high opportunities and lofty estate and became as
the beasts of the field. And the Lord said: "I shall send
thee a redeemer who shall win thee and woo thee, and
teach thee, and bring thee back. And some day thou
shall inherit again that glorious and high estate from
which thou hast fallen." We shall have our Eden, our tree
of life, back again. That's the way the Bible speaks of the
man God made.

There are those who purport to be great teachers and
infallible scientists, who say that this revelation in the
Bible is directly opposite to what actually happened. They
say that out of nothing, out of space, something created
itself. Out of the great vacuum of this space around us
there came this universe. Out of nothing. Nobody made
it. No purpose; no design. It just made itself. Out of
nothing, something came.

They say that out of that something that came out of
nothing, life generated itself. No one made it. No design
in it. It just happened. It accidentally, spontaneously
generated itself. Then out of that little spontaneously
generated speck of protoplasm there evolved, through
the ages, all of the separated forms of life that we read
about in the past, that we see in the rocks, that we see
around us today; there evolved those forms of life, until
man himself was evolved.

So in demonstrating that hypothesis, which many say is

an assured fact, so-called scientists exhibit in the museums
of the world ape-like, fierce-looking, supposed ancestors
of man, and they say: "See, this is the man as he was
one million years ago, and this is the man as he was
seven hundred thousand years ago, and this is the man
as he was three hundred thousand years ago, and here
he is one hundred thousand years ago, and fifty thousand
years ago, and here he is today."

All of us have seen the pictures of the evolving man as
he came from the anthropoid to his present form. All of
us have seen those pictures, I say, and many of us have
seen those exhibits in museums. They construct whole
families of anthropoids and ape-men, and finally come
up to the man of today. They do that with great certainty, and we are overwhelmed and overawed by the
authority of their supposedly scientific evidence for those
demonstrations of the evolution of man.

This address is entitled "The Hoaxes of Anthropology."
It is our thesis that those creatures, wierd and fierce and
ape-like, are nothing but the products of wild imagination
and plaster of Paris, that they are hoaxes, that they are
by no means and in no way a reflection of the actual
truth and of the actual facts.

SCIENCE IS A SACRED COW

One of the most interesting books that has been published in recent years was written by an American scientist named Anthony Standen and entitled, *Science is a
Sacred Cow*. It begins like this,

> When a white-robed scientist, momentarily looking away
> from his microscope or his cyclotron, makes some pronounce-
> ment for the general public, he may not be understood, but
> at least he is certain to be believed. No one ever doubts
> what is said by a scientist. Statesmen, industrialists, ministers
> of religion, civic leaders, philosophers, all are questioned and
> criticized, but scientists, never. Scientists are exalted beings
> who stand at the top-most pinnacle of popular prestige, for

they have a monopoly of the formula, "it has been scientifically proved" which appears to rule out all possibility of disagreement.

Thus the world is divided into scientists, who practice the art of infallibility, and non-scientists, sometimes contemptuously called "laymen," who are taken in by it. The laymen see the prodigious things that science has done, and they are impressed and overawed. . . . Science has achieved so many things . . . that it is hard to believe it can be wrong in anything.

Since it is only human nature to accept such flattery, the scientists accept the laymen's opinion about themselves. The laymen, on the other hand, get their information about scientists from the scientists themselves, and so the whole thing goes 'round and 'round like the whip at Coney Island.

When a fact is a fact, we receive it as a fact. When a truth is a truth, we receive it as a truth. God is light and in Him is no fault or error at all. And the same hand that writes in the sky, the same hand that wrote in the Book, will be the same hand we see in all the forms and facts of life around us.

With the truth we have no quarrel. With a fact we have no quarrel. But this also is a fact: A theory is a theory and a hypothesis is a hypothesis and a guess is a guess. A so-called scientist in supporting his hypothesis can be as blind and as biased as the most superstitious, fanatical animist, and in many, many instances, in the name of so-called science, scientists have perpetrated on the public some of the most enormous and unbelievable hoaxes you could ever read in the story of humanity.

One of the most astounding phenomena in the world today is these exhibits in the great museums, purporting to illustrate and to prove the evolution of man from a lower beast. The so-called evidences for the extended antiquity of man are purely hypothetical, manufactured out of the imagination. Yet they are presented as scientifically, factually, indisputably true. Scientific reputations are used

to perpetuate shams and hoaxes that would make the late
Barnum turn green with envy.

These things that are presented, these so-called ape-
man, are not factual, they are not true. They are figments
of a wild imagination and are contrived through the use
of plaster of Paris. It is our purpose to demonstrate these
hoaxes of anthropology.

These ape-men who are supposed to belong to the
evolutionary ancestry of our humankind are named
after the place where they are supposed to have been discovered. There is the Nebraska Man, the Java Man, the
Peking Man, the Galilee Man, the Piltdown Man, the
Neanderthal Man, and so forth, and so forth. We shall
begin in the order of their age, the oldest first and come
up to the latest.

THE NEBRASKA MAN

The oldest man was supposed to have been the Nebraska Man — "Hespero Pithecus Haroldcookii' — that's his
name. *Hesperos* is the Greek word for "evening," and so
became the Greek word for "western." *Pithecus,* of
course, is the Greek word for "ape." So "Hespero Pithecus" would be "the western ape." And "Haroldcookii" —
we'll see him in a minute.

At the Scopes evolution trial in Dayton, Tennessee,
William Jennings Bryan was confronted with a bevy of
great scientific authorities led by Professor H. H. New-
man of the University of Chicago. The professor astounded Mr. Bryan with the so-called facts of the "Nebraska Man," one of the race of men who dwelt in this
country "one million years ago."

Bryan had no reply, except to say that he thought the
evidence was too scanty to base upon it such far-reaching
conclusions, and Bryan pleaded for more time and for
more data.

But the experts scoffed; they laughed at him, they made

a joke of it. The greatest scientific authorities of the world knew the age of the Nebraska Man was one million years ago.

What was the scientific proof for the Nebraska Man? There was a man by the name of Harold Cook who discovered this famous fossil man and the new race was named after him, "Hespero Pithecus" — "the Western Man" — "Haroldcookii."

A tremendous literature was built up about this fossil race of North America. The most conservative estimate of the age of that race was one million years.

What was this find? Just what did Mr. Harold Cook discover in the state of Nebraska? He discovered a tooth! He discovered *one* tooth! He discovered just one tooth! Not teeth — tooth! This famous tooth was examined by the greatest scientists in the United States, and it was proof positive of a pre-historic race in America and beyond a shadow of a doubt, the man lived here at least one million years ago.

Sir Grafton Elliott Smith induced the editor of the *Illustrated London News* to send a man to America to learn all about this extinct race of humanity and to write an article in the *News*. And in that article were published pictures of a male and a female of this fossilized race that was here in America one million years ago, and they were made on the basis of one tooth!

Dr. William K. Gregory, curator in the American Museum of Natural History, and professor of Paleontology at Columbia University, called it "the million dollar tooth," and he described it as belonging to a human being of such antiquity that a million years in age for it was a conservative estimate.

Dr. Fairfield Osborn, America's greatest paleontologist, in his tremendous address before the American Philosophical Society at Philadelphia, April 27, 1927, placed

"Hespero Pithecus" at the very bottom of the tree depicting the ancestry of man.

Just what was that tooth that Harold Cook discovered in the state of Nebraska, and which created this tremendous certainty on the part of the so-called scientists who scoffed and laughed at William Jennings Bryan with their scientific evidence? Just what was it that Harold Cook discovered?

In the years since the Scopes trial, the skeleton of that entire animal has been discovered. That tooth belonged to a peccary, a species of a pig now extinct in the United States but at one time found all over this continent in large numbers. *It was the tooth of a pig!* And these are the men who laughed at William Jennings Bryan! And these are the men who made a whole race of humanity out of the tooth of a pig long since dead, and who even dated the race of humanity, represented by that tooth, as one million years! That's a hoax of anthropology!

There was advertised in this country and in the world a great discovery called the Southwest Colorado Man. It has been shown since that great advertisement that this new "discovery" was constructed out of the tooth of a horse of the Eocene Period.

"Give us a tooth," cry the experts, "and we will create a whole race of fossilized humanity."

THE JAVA APE-MAN

Now we come to the most famous of all of these anthropoids that are supposed to be in the family of humanity, the Java Ape-Man, Pithecanthropus Erectus. *Pithecus,* remember, is the Greek word for ape. *Anthropus* the Greek word for man, *Erectus* — standing up. So, "Pithecanthropus Erectus" — the ape man who stands up. He is the most famous of all of their find.

In 1891, Dr. Eugene Dubois, an ardent evolutionist, a physician in the Dutch Army then stationed in Java, found in Central Java a small piece of the top of a skull, a fragment of a left thigh-bone, and three molar teeth. They were not found together, but in a range of some fifty or seventy feet. They were not found at the same time, but within the space of a year. They were found in an old river bed mingled with much debris and many bones of extinct animals. The creature lived, the evolutionist says, seven hundred and fifty thousand years ago.

Dr. Chapin, in his book, *Social Evolution*, says: "It was fortunate that the most distinctive portions of the human frame should have been preserved, because from these specimens, we are able to reconstruct the entire being. This man stood half-way between the anthropoid and the existing men."

But when we look at those things, the top of a skull, the fragment of a left thigh-bone and three molar teeth, immediately there are some questions that come to our minds.

From the beginning, the scientists differed greatly about the identification of the bones. Some said they came from a man, some said an ape, some said a baboon, and some said a monkey.

One authority wrote: "Shortly after this discovery, twenty-four of the most eminent scientists of Europe met. Ten said the bones belonged to an ape; seven, to a man; and seven said they were a missing link."

The great Professor Virchow of Berlin, said: "There is no evidence at all that these bones were parts of the same creature."

Even H. G. Wells, the historian who was so greatly disposed in favor of evolution, admitted that the remains were those of an ape, or more probably two apes.

And finally, Dr. Dubois himself, the man who discovered them, and who was the great proponent for their identification as being the bones of the missing link, reversed his opinion as to the missing-link character of his find and

came to the conclusion that the bones were the remains
of some sort of gibbon.

That is the basis for the world-famous "Pithecanthropus
Erectus" found in every museum and in every book as-
serting to describe the lineage of man.

Notice again: those bones were found in sands in a
river bed. Could they have been preserved for seven hundred and fifty thousand years in sand? A petrified skeleton, a skeleton that turns to rock, incased in rock, could
exist there for millions of years. But an unpetrified skeleton, buried in sand, would not last even five thousand
years! And yet we are told these little bones were preserved in sand for seven hundred and fifty thousand years!
Tell me, is this not true? If unpetrified skeletons could last in
sand for seven hundred and fifty thousand years, we would
find them everywhere, billions and billions of them. I say on
the face of it, it is a hoax, another one of the vast hoaxes
of anthropology.

Immediately a great search began for other "Pithecanthropus" in Java. So, there came out, in 1926, in Java,
an article in the *Science Newsletter* entitled, "Jungle
Speaks Again on Man's Pre-human Relatives: A be-
wildered creature, a man, but deeply marked with the
brand of the ape, has emerged at last from the silence
of two hundred and fifty thousand years, and 'Pithecanthropus' at last has a brother."

This "Pithecanthropus" was discovered likewise in the
center of Java. The newspaper article that came out about
"Pithecanthropus" brother read like this: "Perfect Skull of
Prehistoric Man, Missing Link Found. Professor Heber-
lein, of the Netherlands Government Medical Service, has
discovered at Trinal, in Central Java, a complete skull of
the ape-like creature termed by some 'the missing link'
and by science, 'Pithecanthropus Erectus.' Professor Heber-
lein's find, which is complete and sound, will be kept in

Dutch East India, as the transportation of such relics is prohibited."

And what was that marvelous find? It turned out to be the knee-bone of an extinct *elephant!* Another one of the hoaxes of anthropology!

THE HEIDELBERG JAW

We come now to another of the great and famous ape-men who are reconstructed and who are exhibited in the museums and whose pictures you see in books. We come now to the Heidelberg Man, which is actually a Heidelberg jaw.

The Heidelberg jaw was found by Dr. Schoetensack in the *sands* (there it is again), in the sands of the Mauer River, near Heidelberg, Germany. Hence, it is called the Mauer Jaw, or the Heidelberg Jaw, or by the high-sounding Latin name of "Homo" (the Latin word for Man) "Heidelbergensis." First it was said to be seven hundred thousand years old. Later, they said it was only three hundred and seventy-five thousand years old (just any wild guess will do, one's as good as another).

The identification of the jaw-bone also caused great differences of opinion among the anthropologists. Some claimed it to be a connecting link. Others denied it. Some said the find is of utmost value. Others said it is worthless. One scientist said: "These remains show no trace of being intermediate between man and the anthropoid ape."

One distinguished scientist showed that a skull of a modern Eskimo had the same appearance and peculiarities as the Heidelberg Jaw. Another scientist said he had discovered, in the South Pacific, a whole race of South Sea islanders, all of whom have massive jawbones like the "Homo Heidelbergensis." Another scientist said one can walk down the streets of any city and see men everywhere who have Heidelberg jaws, great, heavy, lower jaws.

All it took, then, was plaster of Paris. The features of the ape-like form were made out of sheer imagination and placed in the museum and it was said, "This is a demonstration of the evolution of man."

Another hoax of anthropology, the Heidelberg Jaw!

THE PILTDOWN MAN

The next famous man, coming up in the evolutionary theory is the "Piltdown Man."

In 1912, Charles Dawson, an amateur fossilologist, brought to Dr. Arthur Smith Woodward, eminent paleontologist at the British Museum, some bones and primitive implements he said he found in a gravel pit at Piltdown, Sussex, in the southern part of England. He brought a piece of a jaw, two molar teeth, and a piece of a skull. They were acclaimed by the anthropologists as possibly one-half million years old. Dr. Woodward, in honor of the discoverer, named the creature "Eoanthropus Dawsoni." *Eos* — Greek word for dawn, *anthropus* —man, so "Eoanthropus" is "Dawn-Man" of Sussex, England — the "Piltdown Man."

Oh, what a literature they created on him! How they manufactured him and put him in the museum and made pictures of him for the books! The Encyclopedia Brittanica calls the "Piltdown Man" second only in importance to "Pithecanthropus Erectus."

Henry Fairfield Osborn, the great American paleontologist of the American Museum of Natural History, said: "Eoanthropus — it's darkly-colored and thoroughly-fossilized skull fragments are intermingled with fragments of grinding teeth of Proboscidians, of unquestionable Upper Pliocene age. Eoanthropus, the dawn-man of Sussex, now appears to be of greater geologic age than Pithecanthropus, the Trinal Ape-Man."

On and on they went about the Piltdown Man — Eo-anthropus, from Sussex, England — the Dawn-man. And lo and behold, in the October, 1956 issue of the *Reader's Digest*, was summarized a splendid article from the Popular Science Monthly, entitled "The Great Piltdown Hoax."

The whole hoax was exposed! The jaw-bone was that of an ape that had died only fifty years before. The teeth were filed down to disguise their original design and shape and both teeth and bones were artificially colored with bichromate of potash! Out of that they created the great Piltdown Man and placed him in the museum and put his picture in the books from which we teach our children and to which we have reference on our shelves! Another hoax of anthropology.

THE NEANDERTHAL MAN

Near Dusseldorf, the Dussel River runs through a beautiful little gorge called the Neanderthal Gorge. On one side is a limestone cliff. In that cliff was found a few bones and then controversy started again, this time over a so-called Neanderthal Man. The significance of the discovery of the bones was hotly disputed by the scientists themselves both as to their age, and whether they were human or animal or mere abnormalities.

Here is the point: With these few fragments in each case, an ape-man is reconstructed according to the fancy of the artist who determines posture, stature, size, head, neck, eyes, expression, shape, appearance of skin, hair, whole families. I have seen whole families built, depicting the life and the appearance of these weird creatures. They are *all* imaginatively constructed!

Don't you know it would be impossible to show how a man looked after he had been dead just a few years, if you had only his skeleton? But wild-eyed, imaginative anthropologists create these weird creatures by the thousand. It is estimated that there are three hundred replicas of the Piltdown Man in museums around the world. It is estimated that nearly one million persons annually pass through the American Museum of Natural History in New York and view, according to the artist's fancy, the reconstruction of Pithecanthropus, the Heidelberg Man, the Piltdown Man, and the Neanderthal Man, the "ancestors of the human race." And the multitude of high school teachers and students, as well as the general public are never told how dubious and unscientific the representations are. They are pawned off in the name of science as being actual and factual, and they are nothing but hoaxes of anthropology.

I have three observations to make, and the first observation is this: The term "missing-link" is a colossal misnomer. The scientist Anthony Standen in *Science Is a Sacred Cow* said: "It is a most misleading phrase because it suggests that only one link is missing. It would be more accurate to say that the greater part of the chain is missing, so much that it is not entirely certain whether there is a chain at all."

"The first link is missing." Where did that life come from? And every intermediate link between is missing. Not one has been found.

Here are statements made by some of the great scientists of the world. Professor Branco, of Berlin University: "Man appeared suddenly in the Quaternary period. Paleontology tells us nothing on the subject. It knows no ancestors of man."

Erich Wassmann, in *Modern Biology and the Theory of Evolution*: "The whole hypothetical pedigree of man is not supported by a single fossil genus of a single fossil species."

Professor Virchow of Berlin: "The man-ape has no existence and the missing link remains a phantom."

Austin H. Clark, biologist of the Smithsonian Institution: "Missing links are mis-representations."

Professor Wm. L. Straus, Jr., in the *Quarterly Review of Biology*: "It is noteworthy, moreover, that forms intermediate between the human and any other primate groups, forms popularly termed 'missing links,' are as conspicuous by their absence as they were one hundred years ago."

Professor Rendle Short: "The further back we look for early man, the more like ourselves he appears to be."

The second observation is this: The arrangements, through so-called evolutionary ages, based on forms of bones and instruments used, can be vastly misleading. And I mean by that this:

In our present day some of us drive automobiles, or ride in jet planes, while down in Ecuador are savages who live in the old stone age. There are different grades of cultures and degrees of civilization throughout this earth. Now suppose all of us were buried in mud, and one hundred million years from now, if the world should last, men should dig down and find our fossilized forms. Wouldn't the evolutionists have a case! There they would find the Ecuadorian Indian with his stone tools. Then they would find the Eskimos, and the head-hunters, and the Arabs, and the Mongolians, and they would find us. They would put us all in an exhibit and say, "See, this is evolution! There you have the Eskimos, the Arab, the Mongolian, and the man driving the jet plane. See, that demonstrates evolution." It does not demonstrate any such thing! We were all contemporary here together! Some of us had higher degrees of civilization than others. But we did not evolve out of one another.

Now the third and the last observation is this: If there is any change in the human race itself, it seems to me it is down and not up. These great races of the past were greatest physically. Years and years and years ago, there lived "Cro-Magnon-Man," every one of them beautifully formed, and every one of them over six feet tall. They lived thousands and thousands of years ago. The race thousands and thousands of years ago was stronger physically than it is now.

If it changes it is going down. Giant's teeth, sold in shops in China, are teeth of a race of men who lived thousands of years ago, and every one of them was over seven feet tall, tremendous specimens. If we are going anywhere, physically, we are going down. We are not coming up. The great physical specimen of humanity is not today. It was thousands of years ago.

I say the same thing, intellectually. Thousands of years ago, the world had Aristotle and Plato and Socrates. There has never been any group of men that has come up to the great intellectuals of those Greeks who lived in the golden period of Pericles — and that was thousands of years ago.

Spiritually, if there is any change in the human race, it is degeneration, it is devolution. It is not up and out and on, it is down and down and down. Where is the giant with God who can sing songs as David sang them? Where are the giant men of God like Isaiah the prophet, who could see hundreds of years and predict as though he stood by the occasion, the great thing that was coming to pass?

Evolution says it is up and up and up, and by and by we will produce super men. The theory says we came from the beasts and we shall be angels tomorrow. Jesus Christ lived two thousand years ago. So did John and Peter and Paul. It seems to me that if we are going in any direction it is the other way, not up.

THE DUBIOUS DEFENSES OF DARWINISM

CHAPTER 7

THE DUBIOUS DEFENSES OF DARWINISM

WE READ IN GENESIS 1:26, 27 and 2:7:

And God said, Let us make man in our image, after our
likeness . . . So God created man in his own image, in the
image of God created he him; male and female created he them
. . . And the Lord God formed man out of the dust of the
ground, and breathed into his nostrils the breath of life; and man
became a living soul.

This is the record of the Genesis account of the creation
of man.

It has been our thesis that all the facts of biology,
embryology, paleontology, fossilology and anthropology
support this act of special creation. It has been our thesis
that there is no known, discoverable, demonstrable fact
that denies this special creation by the hand of God.

The evolutionist, the materialist, faces a staggering
and colossal problem with reference to this little speck
of life he says evolved out of nothing and finally evolved
into man. He faces a staggering problem in demonstrating such a hypothesis.

In fact, it is so staggering that when he seeks to give
an answer in demonstration, there are as many theories
and hypotheses of the evolutionary process as there are
evolutionists themselves. The only thing they agree on
is this: God had nothing to do with the evolutionary
process, but it blindly, accidentally, evolved of itself.

The predecessor of Charles Darwin was the French
scientist Lamarck. He noticed all of the different vari-

eties, shapes, sizes, and colors among the parents of the
different forms of life. He concluded that environment
changed the offspring and they in turn bequeathed these
acquired characteristics to their progeny, and so gradually and finally, new species developed.

As late as 1900, biologists believed that acquired characteristics — something a parent acquires during his life-
time — were inheritable. Take a dog, cut off his tail, and
its puppies will not have tails. That is an example of an
acquired characteristic. Now, of course, we know that
such a hypothesis is unthinkable.

Acquired characteristics are not inheritable. If you
cut off your hand, your child will be born with two
hands just the same. Whatever happens to you, the
child's inheritance does not come from any characteristic
that you may have acquired. When the sperm and the
egg are united, its inheritance is therein forever sealed.

Charles Darwin followed Lamarck. And he did so with
the remark, "May heaven forfend me from Lamarck's nonsense." He started on an altogether different plane, and
from an altogether different basis. He believed that all the
different forms of life which culminated in man evolved
from one low beginning.

For example, here is a quotation from Charles Darwin:

"Our most ancient progenitors in the kingdom of the
vertebrata, at which we are able to obtain an obscure
glance, apparently consisted of a group of marine animals resembling the larvae of the existing ascidians"
(little worms in the water). Then he suggests a line
of ascent from those little worms to the monkey and
finally to the man.

As Charles Darwin worked out his theories of evolution of how the ascent of man came about, he hit
upon two great laws. First, he says it came about by
the operation of natural selection or the survival of the

fittest. And second, it came about through the operation of the law of sexual selection.

So, we are going to look at those two great Darwinian laws of evolution.

THE SURVIVAL OF THE FITTEST

We will take first the law of natural selection, the law of the survival of the fittest.

Darwin noticed two things as he looked over the life-forms of the world. First, he noticed that the offspring of parents differ among themselves from the parents. Sometimes they differ in size, sometimes they differ in shape. But there are differences among the offspring of the common parent. Kittens may have different colors; puppies may have different sizes, and on and on. That is seen everywhere. Darwin noticed those varieties in the offspring as compared to the parents.

The second thing he noticed was that there was a struggle for existence on the part of these myriad of offspring that are born into the world. Not all of the acorns grow into trees; not all the eggs of the fish grow into fishes. There are a great many more acorns and a great many more eggs than ever actually develop into mature parents. So, Darwin concluded that there was a vast struggle for existence among the many different species that are born into this world.

Now, from those two observations he deduced this first law, that the fittest survive, that by the accumulation, through the ages and ages, of minute modification, new organs developed and new species came into being. Those that were not advantageous were rigidly rejected, deemed unfit to survive; only those survived that were the strongest and fittest; the rest perished.

Now, the basis of that law, when we begin to apply it, is this: The new organs and the new species gradually evolved through an accumulation of slight modifications. Those little differences, when they were added, gradually developed into the new species.

This theory seems learned and smart when one looks at it. As long as it is theoretical it seems to demonstrate keen insight. But when one begins to apply it to the actual development of a new organ, it is an astonishing hypothesis.

When we try to explain the development of an eye (there was a time when there were no eyes, according to theory), when we apply it to the development of a heart (there was a time when there were no hearts), when we begin to apply it to the development of an ear (there was a time when there were no ears), when we begin to apply it to the development of a leg, or a lung (there was a time when there were no lungs and no legs), when we begin to apply the hypothesis to the actual development of the organ, it becomes an astonishing thing.

For example, let us take the eye. There was a time of course, according to the evolutionists, when there were no eyes. We all began as a tiny speck of protoplasm that gradually evolved.

Then where did that eye come from? Well, according to the evolutionists it came like this: Upon the body of the creature, ages ago, there was a pimple, or a freckle, or a pigment of skin. And when the light shone on the creature, it was a little more sensitive where the pimple, or the freckle, or the pigment was on the skin. So the creature turned that freckle to the sunlight and as the waves of light beat upon that freckle, through millions and millions and uncounted millions of years, it gradually, being irritated, became a sensitive spot, and that sensitive spot through the centuries, gradually developed a nerve, and that irritated nerve gradually turned into an eye. That is where your eye came from.

How could that one pimple, or that one freckle, or that one pigment, stay in the same place through millions and millions and uncounted millions of years, while that eye was developing?

According to the theory, there had to be another pimple, and another freckle, and another pigment in the skin because you have two eyes and not one.

Is it not a remarkable thing that they just happen to be in the right place! Not on the bottom of your foot or on the top of your head, but on each side of your nose, just right!

Is it not an unusual thing that there happened to be just two! As those waves of light played on the freckle, why did those eyes not develop all over the body? Is it not a marvelous thing that it quit developing! We do not see it anymore! Why do we not see eyes in the process of developing now? The theory is an astonishing thing when we apply it to the development of any organ of the body.

Aren't you glad that when the light waves played on another freckle it turned into an ear? Aren't you glad the ears were placed just right, and not crooked, and not just anywhere on your body? Wasn't that a fortunate thing?

Where did your legs come from? Well, says the evolutionists, there was a time, of course, when there were not any legs. And in the days when there were not any legs, there was a creature that had a wart on it, and as the creature went along, he found out by leaning on that wart, and shoving with that wart, he could move just a little better and faster. So he came to depend upon that wart as he moved himself along. And by and by, through the uncounted millions of years, that wart turned into a leg.

Is it not fortunate that there was another wart in just the right place, and that it turned into a leg?

When I read all that, I thought, *We have been evolving*

in the wrong direction. A man has just two legs. There are other animals that have four legs. And I know of an animal I am told has one hundred legs. Looks like we are going in the wrong direction!

Did you know that if anything as idiotic as that were in the Bible it would be scoffed at endlessly? It would be laughed at forever. And yet these are the truths, these are the facts of so-called scientific evolution! It insults the intelligence of any ordinary man!

Inexplicable Contradictions

Now, Darwin had access to one other appeal in bolstering his theory of the accumulation of minute advantages that finally developed into organs and into new species. He appealed to geological time. He said: "Now these things could not come to pass in a few years or in a few million years. But, they developed over ages and ages." For example, in one of Charles Darwin's calculations, he came to the astonishing conclusion that 306,662,400 years was a "mere trifle" in the evolutionary process. Three hundred and six million years!

All school boys know that in the vast ages of the past this world, this earth, this planet, has changed in its surface and in its climate many, many times. Darwin has to assume that this world was in its present condition for millions and millions of years in order for the evolutionary process to develop. And any school boy knows that this world has not been in its present condition, favorable to the life that you now see, for anything like that period of time.

I would think that all the biologists are now persuaded that the period of life on this earth is not nearly so long as men once thought it was. Life has just not been here on this planet nearly as long as these vast geological ages deemed necessary by Darwin.

Another point about the theory of natural selection

and the survival of the fittest is: The law itself, as stated by Darwin, is contradictory. This is Darwin's law as he states it: "This preservation of favorable individual differences and variations and the destruction of those which are injurious, I have called natural selection, or the survival of the fittest . . . any variation in the least degree injurious would be rigidly destroyed."

There is a violent contradiction in the law itself. First, Darwin says that all of these organs and all of these species were developed by the gradual accumulation of favorable, minute, advantageous modifications. Then, he says in the next sentence that any modification that was injurious, that was not usable, would be rigidly rejected. If these organs are useless until they are complete, the law of natural selection would immediately and rigidly reject them as being unfit to survive. So how did they develop? How could they?

Now, let me apply this law and you can see it more easily. Let us take a spider. In the posterior region of the spider are highly specialized organs for the spinning of a web. He spins the web in order to gain food to eat, that he might live. Now, in the millions, and millions, and millions of years it took for those modifications in the posterior regions of the spider to develop into those highly specialized organs, so he could spin a web, so he could catch his food and eat, why did he not starve to death while those organs were developing so he could spin his web?

Now, if he ate some other way (and he had to eat some other way) then those little modifications that finally developed into spinning organs would have been rigidly rejected. Those little modifications would have been deemed unfit to live. There would have been no point in their development if the spider were already eating some other way, so they would never have come to pass.

Let us take this theory again and apply it to the mammary glands. The breasts of the mammals (which, we are told, are the highest in the order of the evolutionary process) are the means by which the mammals feed their young.

In the millions and millions of years while those mammary glands were developing how is it that the young were fed? Why did they not starve to death? If the young were fed some other way, how is it that those mammary glands developed? They were supposedly useless for millions and millions of years, until they were mature. And in those years that they were developing, those modifications would have been useless. According to Darwin's own law, any variation that was useless would be rigidly destroyed.

The sexual organs had to develop simultaneously and parallel in the male and in the female. So while they were developing in the male, through millions and millions of years, and while they were developing in the female, through millions and millions of years, they were useless until they were fully developed and could complement each other. Now, in those millions and millions of years, while those modifications were being developed, any variation in the least degree useless would have been rigidly destroyed. How did they ever finally develop?

The law has in it a violent contradiction, and when we apply it to the development of a new organ or to the development of a new species, we come into an absolutely impossible vacuum. We cannot help but agree with Professor Lock of Cambridge who said: "Selection, whether natural or artificial, can have no power in creating anything new."

Hugh de Vries declared: "Natural selection may explain the *survival* of the fittest, but it cannot explain the *arrival* of the fittest."

Professor Coultre, of the University of Chicago said:

"The most fundamental objection to the theory of natural selection is that it cannot originate character; it only selects among characters already existing."

And yet, the law of the survival of the fittest is the great basic law of evolution. When you apply it and look at it, it is a ridiculous thing and almost unintelligible!

SEXUAL SELECTION

Darwin has one other law. He found that he could not by any means explain all of the phenomena of the forms of life by his first law, that of natural selection through the survival of the fittest. He found that there are some things, some characteristics of man, for example, that could only be explained by plain, conscious choice. So he promulgated his second law, that of sexual selection.

Now, he applied that to two things among others:

First, in Darwin's day it was the accepted theory that a man's mind was superior to a woman's mind; that male intelligence was finer and stronger than a woman's intelligence. In Darwin's day people believed that, so Darwin had to explain it.

Another thing Darwin sought to explain by the principle of sexual selection is this: It was true in Darwin's day, it was true from the beginning of man, and it is true today that man is born a hairless, uncovered animal. Now, what advantage was it for a man to evolve naked from a heavily-covered anthropoid? He is the only animal in the world that has no covering. He has to make one for himself. To every other animal in the world God has given a covering! But not to the man. How was that an advantage that he came to be naked?

Darwin explains all this by sexual selection. He explains the supposed superiority of the male mind over the female mind by saying that the male struggled for the female and, therefore, in the struggle he developed a mind superior to the female's. And that is why the man has mental intelligence superior to that of the woman.

His explanation of why the man is hairless is this: The women preferred anthropoids with less hair. Consequently, they bred the hair off of the men. Now, when you read all this you go in circles. Darwin has just said that the mental superiority of the man came about because of the man's choice of the female. Then in the next page he says the reason the man is naked is because of the female's choice of the male who had less hair. Just which one is actually choosing which?

My observation would be this: Females then were doubtless not different from females now. They have always differed in their taste, don't you think? Some of them would like a big anthropoid brute with a slick, heavy coat of hair all over him. Others would like the hair a little less heavy and thick.

When Darwin published a later edition of his *Descent of Man* where he spoke of these things, he fortified that theory. He reiterated the supposed fact that the reason a man was born a hairless animal was because of the female choice. The female liked him with less hair. His added proof was that there had been reported to him that there was a mandrill (another name for a ferocious West African baboon) that was proud of a bare spot on his body. And that is proof for this supposition that the female took the hair off the male by choosing men who had less hair! Reading the minds of baboons can be precarious business!

I repeat, if such insanity, if such silliness, if such ridiculousness were in the Bible, you would laugh it to scorn! But this is science! These are the facts of evolution!

Let me tell you something; if there is any one thing true about sexual selection it is this: It doesn't evolve upward. It inevitably degenerates. That is true everywhere.

By careful, intelligent selection, by breeding upward the fine points, we finally produce wonderful strains in botany and zoology. But when man tires and quits, the dog turns to a mongrel. The cat turns to a vagabond. The potatoes are too small to dig. The horses are too wild and scrawny to catch and break. The beef cattle turn to ribs and horns. When the string breaks, the kite falls.

It is not evolution upward, this thing of sexual selection, it is degeneration downward! And there is no exception to that in the facts of biology!

DROSOPHILA

In our contemporary, modern day, there has been one other tremendous effort to bolster up the sagging fortunes of Darwinian evolution and it is this: The "Darwinists" have just about admitted that it is hard to demonstrate the evolution of an organ and the evolution of species through the accumulation of minute variations and modifications. So they hit upon the idea that maybe the organs did not evolve through the countless ages — for one thing, those ages in which they could evolve did not exist — but that they came suddenly with a rush of mutations. So in order to demonstrate, the "Darwinists" took the common banana fly — the fruit fly — Drosophila — and began working on him. They found out that by exposing a Drosophila parent fruit fly to the gamma rays of some kind of radioactive material, his mutation — that is, change variation — was speeded up one hundred and fifty times.

So, for more than forty years now, the "Darwinists" have been breeding banana flys and subjecting them to gamma rays to increase the fly's mutation.

What has happened in the corresponding span of Drosophila over these forty years? The "Darwinists" have been breeding them under gamma rays every way they know how to change and mutate those genes. What has the answer been? Has the Drosophila turned into a bumblebee? Has it changed into a June bug?

I had a friend who was working on his doctor's degree in biology and genetics at the University of Texas and he lived with those flys. Wherever he went he had those flys with him. Whatever he was doing he had those flys with him. In the middle of something we were doing, he would have to go see about those flys. He never got away from those flys.

What has been the result? Because of those rays, there are Drosophila with red eyes, there are Drosophila with black eyes, there are Drosophila with little wings, there are Drosophila with big wings. There is Drosophila himself, smaller. There are all kinds of Drosophila and they breed him back and forth, back and forth and change him up and down and again and again, but after one thousand generations and forty years, and after mutants under those gamma rays one hundred and fifty times multiplied, he is still the same Drosophila that the geneticist started with long ago. He doesn't change. That is according to the fixed law of God.

ANCIENT MATERIALISM

Evolution, the speculation of materialism, is not a new thing. It is as old as the human race itself. In the beginning, when men began to think and to write and to turn away from God, they began to speculate on evolution. But physical instruments can never reach into great spiritual reality. Physical science can never penetrate into the origin of anything; it can only observe things that are passing before it in review.

In the dim ages of the past, the Egyptian, the Hindu and the Polynesian had their theories of evolution. They believed that there was a primary egg out of which life was born and out of which life evolved. The Polynesian had to have a bird to lay his egg and the Egyptian and Hindu had to have deity to create the egg. But out of it they believed all of these forms of life evolved.

The ancient Greeks, when they began to philosophize, reviewed that very thing, the evolution of life. It is an old, old speculation. It is an old, old doctrine. It is nothing modern and nothing new. As the ancient Greek philosophers listened to the Hindu doctrine of the transmigration of the soul from animal to animal and finally up to man, they must have gleaned from that the evolving forms of life.

Thales of Miletus, born in 624 B.C., promulgated the idea that everything evolved out of water.

Aniximandes, born in Miletus, 611 B.C., thought everything evolved itself out of pristine mud.

Anixinimus, born in 588 B.C., thought air was the mother of all things.

Heraclitis thought that a soul could only come out of a pure substance like fire.

All of these speculations were summed up in a poem written just before the Christian era by the Roman Epicurean poet Lucretius. It was entitled "De Rerum Natura" or "The Nature of Things." In that poem the author has the atomic theory about as we have it today, and he says that in the many motions of those atoms, there gradually formed the forms and processes of life such as we see it today.

Modern speculation has added nothing new to the ancients. They said it all thousands of years ago. It is a mystery, the birth of any human soul. How we were made and how God created us is a mystery in the great hands of God Himself. Any learned man in this earth knows that evolution is sheer speculation. The great scientist Dr. Rudolph Virchow, of Berlin University, pled with his fellow scientists not to teach the theory of evolution as fact because, he said, it is insupportable and not capable of demonstration. Any intelligent and learned man knows that. In the struggle that ensued, someone lighted the fire and the conflagration began. It reminds us of Titus, who gave orders not to burn the temple in Jerusalem in 70 A.D. But a Roman soldier threw a lighted torch through a small window and the temple caught fire and turned into dust and ashes.

That is what has happened to the academic world of our generation. Through this materialistic philosophy we have a dead, ashen faith in God that has destroyed the hope of myriads.

May the Lord give us learning and wisdom and intelligence as we read. Look in the Book. Look in the Book of Life; look in the book of nature and see there the moving, marvelous, creative hand of God.

THE MARVELOUS MYSTERY OF MAN

CHAPTER 8

THE MARVELOUS MYSTERY OF MAN

> And God said, Let us make man in our image, after our likeness . . . So God created man in his own image, in the image of God created he him; male and female created he them . . . And the Lord God formed man of the dust of the ground, and breathed into his nostrils the breath of life; and man became a living soul (Gen. 1:26, 27; 2:7).

THE WONDER OF THAT creative workmanship is not alone in the Garden of Eden. Nor is it a miracle of the beginning of the human family. A man's body is the most marvelous physical creation in the universe. The making of a star, of a continent, of an ocean, is not to be compared with the wonder of the skill that entered into the making of a man's body.

But this miracle that was wrought by the skillful, infinitely wise and adroit hands of God, in the beginning, in the Garden of Eden, is repeated every day, everywhere. We do not have to look back to that faraway age to wonder at the creative masterpiece of God. The Lord brings to pass the same miracle every day, in place after place.

In Psalm 139:13-16, David mentions this fearful and wonderful miracle of God:

> Thou hast covered me in my mother's womb. I am fearfully and wonderfully made. . . . My substance was not hid from thee, when I was made in secret, and curiously wrought in the lowest parts of the earth. Thine eyes did see my substance, yet being unperfect; and in thy book all my members were written, which in continuance were fashioned, when as yet there was none of them.

111

This is the marvelous mystery of the man.

A man's body may be likened to a vast city, and on the inside of that city are ten times thirty trillions of inhabitants. Ten hundred thousand is a million; ten hundred million is a billion; ten hundred billion is a trillion. Ten times thirty trillion little citizens on the inside of that vast city, all of them with a task assigned. So tiny are those citizens that in one speck of blood no bigger than the head of a pin, there will be five million of them. The three hundred trillion are busy all the time doing their part to operate this infinitely intricate machinery.

THE CELL

Those living units that form this marvelous creative workmanship we call the man, are cells. And each cell is filled with the most amazing, remarkable and marvelous substance in this universe — protoplasm.

The cell is made like this: First, there is a cell wall. The containing cube has a membrane which is pervious. Some things can go through the cell wall, some things can come out of it and other things are prohibited. The tiny cell wall is a marvel in itself.

Then on the inside of that cell wall is a substance called cytoplasm. In the cytoplasm are infinitely small spaces filled with molecules of fluid, of proteins, of sugar and of salt.

But the most miraculous of all the miraculous things in that little cell is the tiny sphere called the nucleus that floats in the cytoplasm. That is the center of life. On the inside of the nucleus are small chromatin granules, and in the process of mitosis or cell division, those chromatin granules gather together into rods called chromosomes.

Every distinct family, every one of the unbreakable species God has made has its distinguishing number of chromosomes, and on those chromosomes a distinguishing number of genes. Drosophila, the comman fruit fly, with which geneticists have been experimenting for half a century, has four chromosomes and on each of those four chromosomes are from twelve to fifteen thousand genes. Those genes have to do with heredity and the building of the body.

The distinguishing number of chromosomes in the cells of man is forty-eight. All of those billions and billions of cells in the human body have forty-eight chromosomes in the nucleus of each one. Some have estimated that on those forty-eight chromosomes in the nucleus of a man there may be as many as eight hundred million genes that have to do with the building of the body.

In the nucleus of each cell in the woman, there are two chromosomes that are different; they are called "XX" chromosomes.

In the man the two that are different are "XY."

In the female reproductive cell, when those chromosomes are halved for the egg cell, there will be one X chromosome in each female egg (twenty-four chromosomes, one of them an X).

In the male germ, however, when the reproductive cell is created, and the chromosomes are divided in half, there will be twenty-four in one cell, one of them an X, and twenty-four in the other cell, but one of them a Y. When they are mated, there will be twenty-four from the female, twenty-four from the male, and again there will be the complete number of forty-eight chromosomes. If the twenty-four from the female with the X chromosome are fertilized by twenty-four from the male with the X chromosome, the new life will be female. But if the twenty-four from the female are fertilized with the twenty-four from the male with the Y chromosome, the new life will be male.

BUILDING A BODY

So without teaching and without training, those marvelous, infinitesimally small genes and chromosomes and cells begin their long and eventful journey building the marvelous body of the marvelous man.

Some of the units seem to be leaders and directors and some of them seem to obey orders, which they do faithfully, immediately and meticulously. Some of those tiny citizens seem to be masons, some carpenters, some plasterers, some generals, some workmen, some doctors, some lawyers, some merchants, some sailors, some policemen, some soldiers. Without direction and without previous experience, without training, they begin to build this marvelous structure we call the man.

Within the first few weeks, in one corner, there are some pumping engineers who begin to construct a simple, one-chambered heart that begins to beat and to pump fluid.

About the same time, the plumbers are laying down all kinds of pipelines from that one-chambered heart the engineers have constructed, and the pump begins to pump fluid through those pipelines. When looked at closely, the system is like a moving cafeteria or a conveyer belt on which are all kinds of things to eat so all of those carpenters and plumbers and electricians can have their food laid right at their door.

Then, within about two months, out of nowhere, there appear the bone-builders, beginning to lay down their structures, the way a man builds a great skyscraper.

Then there appear the teeth carpenters, and they begin to gather materials for the enamel and for the dentine and for the cement and for all the things that go into the laying down of teeth buds. They say, "When the teeth are needed they will be right on time." Everything is done according to schedule, with nothing missing, nothing delayed.

They work and work and by three months, everyone is on the job. Everything is teeming and everything is busy. There are the bone builders gathering calcium and phosphorus in the right proportions and laying it down for the building of the skeleton. There are the plumbers laying all of those thousands and thousands of miles of pipeline. Then there are the electricians and they are laying down their cables all through the body in order that it may have a fine communication system. There are those most marvelous of all tissues, the endocrine glands that are beginning to manufacture their hormones, messenger boys to be sent into any part of this marvelous body. Then there are the power machines — the muscles — that are being rigged up and made ready to work to generate power. They are being tied to all of the bones. Then from the photographic department and from the auditory department the technicians of photography and the technicians of the auditory system are called in and they begin to construct the most marvelous camera in this world, the cornea, the lens and the tiny muscle around that lens, the retina, and then the optic nerve. For protection an eyelid is built and on the inside a smooth membrane. Then on the outer side a little water fountain is constructed by which the delicate eye, that photographic piece, can be constantly washed and bathed and kept meticulously clean.

After everyone has done his part and all the little workmen, without teaching and without training, have all done their work, upon a day the physician and the father and the family and the neighbors and the friends hear the cry of a new-born baby. God has done it again!

Can you imagine the wonder, the miracle? You don't have to go back to Eden. You don't have to go back to the beginning, for before your eyes is the most marvelous, inexplainable mystery in this created universe.

But we haven't started!

THE MYSTERY OF GROWTH

We enter the mystery of growth. What makes that child turn into a man? What makes him grow? No one knows. But the days pass and there he is, growing and growing and growing. What tells him when to stop? His head will grow to the right size, then it will stop. His heart will grow to the right size and then stop. His arms will grow just to the right size and then stop. His feet and his legs will grow to their right size and then stop. Who tells them how long and how big and when to stop? No one knows. It is one of the mysteries of the marvelous man.

THE PROBLEMS OF ANATOMY

Where can a man buy a cap for his knee
 Or a key to the lock of his hair?
Can his eyes be called an academy
 Because there are pupils there?

What gems are found in the crown of his head?
 Who crosses the bridge of his nose?
Can he use when shingling the roof of his house
 The nails on the end of his toes?

Can the crook on his elbow be sent to jail:
 If so what can he do?
How does he sharpen his shoulder-blades
 I'm sure I don't know, do you?

Can he sit in the shade of the palms of his hands
 Or beat on the drum of his ear?
Does the calf of his leg eat the corn on his toes?
 If so, why not grow corn on the ear?

As the child grows and turns into man, think of the marvelous mystery of change and supply and rebuilding and reconstruction. It goes on fabulously, enormously, miraculously. Every minute and moment of every week of every month of every year of the whole life, the entire body, all of it, is being marvelously rebuilt. Solid bone, piece by piece (the way workers take timbers out of a railroad bridge), is being torn down and reconstructed. Every unit of the eye is being taken apart and rebuilt, yet it never loses a moment of life. The steam is never cut off, the electricity is never shut down. It never stops.

Each little workman comes in, picks up where his predecessor has been working and carries right on without a moment's hesitation.

This is an amazing thing! We have to have new brains, but we are never conscious of any change. We have to have new lungs, but we never lose a breath. We have to have new stomachs, but we never lose a meal. We have to have new hearts, but they never cease to beat. All of this marvelous work is being changed piece by piece every moment of every day and every night, and we never realize it, nor are we conscious of it at all.

Could you think of a factory like that where even the operator was not conscious of the changes in his factory, and yet his factory is being rebuilt from top to bottom?

The most amazing thing about these cells that inhabit by the millions and billions this house we call the body of man, is their know-how. Their knowledge is astounding. It is the knowledge of God Himself. Such unbelievable things these cells know how to do!

Let us take some of them, for example. What a marvelous chemical know-how enters into the manufacture of blood. In an ordinary, healthy man, there is about a gallon and one-half of blood. On the inside of that blood, there are at least thirty trillion red cells called corpuscles. They die, they are injured, they are destroyed at the rate of about seventy-two million a minute, so they have to be replaced. They have to be remade at the rate of seventy-two million a minute!

THE CHEMICAL FACTORIES

How is a red corpuscle made? On the inside of that tiny corpuscle is a red substance called hemoglobin. It is a protein and has a vast capacity for oxygen. When it comes to the lungs it grabs all the oxygen that it can possibly care for, four times as much as itself, and then takes it down to all those living cells that have to have it to breathe and live. Did you ever try to make a piece of hemoglobin? I want you to look at the miraculous chemical know-how of these factories that create hemoglobin. A molecule of water is made of two atoms of hydrogen and one atom of oxygen — H_2O — that's water. Carbon dioxide would be made of one atom of carbon and two atoms of oxygen. One molecule of glucose, which is body sugar, would be made out of six atoms of carbon, twelve atoms of hydrogen and six atoms of oxygen ($C_6H_{12}O_6$). One molecule of some fats would be eighteen atoms of carbon, thirty-six atoms of hydrogen, three atoms of oxygen ($C_{18}H_{36}O_2$). Now, one molecule of hemoglobin, that scarlet red protein on the inside of that little cell (and there are three hundred million molecules of this chemical on the inside of the cell) is $C_{758}H_{1203}N_{195}S_3Fe_1O_{218}$, which means one molecule of this red hemoglobin has in it 758 atoms of carbon, 1203 atoms of hydrogen, 195 atoms of nitrogen, 3 atoms of sulphur, 1 atom of iron and 218 atoms of oxygen, making a total in each molecule of hemoglobin of 2378 atoms. Now molecules of hemoglobin have to be made exactly like that. If they are not, they are something else.

Those red cells are made at the rate of seventy-two million a minute. Can you imagine the job of the chemist who had to take our 758 atoms of carbon, 1203 atoms of hydrogen, 195 atoms of nitrogen, 3 atoms of sulphur, 1 atom of iron, 218 atoms of oxygen, and count them up — 300 million to the cell, 72 million cells to the minute? And yet the bone marrow cells do it like the snap of a finger all the time!

Where is the chemist who can do that? Yet those little factories do that day and night, silently, unobtrusively, skillfully, and we never realize it.

Where are the little factories? Just as a bank vault is put down in the foundations of a building, so the all-wise architectural Designer and Engineer put those factories in the most protected parts of the human frame, deep down on the inside of the marrow of the bone. There we find those little factories coining out cells, counting out atomic numbers in the right proportion and manufacturing them by the millions and the billions every minute. What an amazing process, what God hath done!

A chemist can pretty well figure out what is in hemoglobin. But there are other little chemical factories in the body that have knowledge to construct things that no human mind in this earth can enter into. So delicate, so intricate, so deep, so unfathomable are they, that no one knows what they are or how they are made.

For example, does anyone know what an enzyme is, how it is made, how it is constructed? An enzyme is an organic piece of matter that can change other things but is not changed itself. It can take starch, for example, and change it into sugar. What are those enzymes, how are they constructed and how are they manufactured? What is their component part and what is on the inside of them? The answer is known but to God Himself.

Again, I do not know of anything that is more amazing than the creation of the ductless glands, called the endocrine glands.

You have two kinds of glands in your body — you have a duct gland that will pour out its secretions through a pipe in a designated place in your body. An example of a duct gland is the gall bladder. But there are in your body marvelous little pieces of tissue that are the most amazing pieces of tissue in this earth. You have in your body pieces of tissue that secrete chemicals which are poured directly into the blood stream, which in turn carries them wherever they are needed. These chemicals carry messages to tell the different parts of the body what to do.

The activity of your body is regulated by two means.

One is the nervous system. Little cables and wires of communication go all over your body from the spinal column, providing one way for body activity to be coordinated. The other way your body activity is coordinated is through these messengers that are secreted by the endocrine glands.

Until recently, evolutionists looked at the endocrine glands and said: "Why they are just vestigial remnants. They were useful in the day when man was a beast. But now since the ape has evolved upward, they are useless and these are just the remnants of those useless organs that he once had to have."

They did not know why the beast had to have them. They did not know what function they served. The evolutionist did not see any reason for these glands, so he said they were vestigial remnants. They were doubtless useful to the beast, but to the man they are not useful at all. That is typical of the evolutionist's reasoning and it is also typical of what happens to his argument when we finally know the facts. These glands are in no wise remnants. The most important tissues in our bodies are the endocrine glands, and we are just beginning to find that out. Far from being remnants, they were put there by the marvelous creative hand of God Himself.

The adrenal glands above the kidneys are sometimes called the glands of flight and fight. They are there for preserving life.

If something scares you and you have to jump, the adrenal gland will send a hormone messenger to the liver and the liver will immediately turn loose glycogen that is immediately turned into glucose, into blood sugar, and the muscles are ready to work. Then the adrenal gland will send a hormone messenger to all of the little blood vessels of the body. They constrict and more blood-pressure results. Then the adrenal gland will send a hormone messenger to the heart and the heart muscle is toned up and is ready to do twice as much work. The adrenal gland will manufacture a hormone messenger and send it through the blood stream to the pupil of the eye which is dilated. You are then ready for fight or for flight. The manufacture of the chemical of that gland is a marvel!

No one in this earth understands how a muscle is made, or how it moves. Man has already discovered fifteen chemical reactions in the functioning of a muscle. One enzyme will take what the other has done and work on that, then another enzyme will come and take that product and change it until finally energy is liberated. How? no one knows. And yet an athlete can jump his height and a skilled violinist and a fine pianist can use their fingers and arms almost automatically. But the reaction, the chemical reaction, of just moving a muscle is just beyond any man's reasoning.

We have not even begun. Oh, that I could speak of the mystery of the mind, the mystery of memory and the mystery of the human soul. The greatest spiritual creation in this earth is a man's soul, his mind, his memory, his personality, the spirit that resides within him, "And man became a living soul."

When the silver cord is loosed
When the golden bowl is broken
When the pitcher is broken at the fountain
And the wheel is broken at the cistern
When the dust returns to the earth as it was
And the spirit unto God who gave it.

Oh, the marvelous mystery of the man. We can but bow our heads and humble our hearts in the presence of the great Designer and Creator and architect Who made us and fashioned us in His own likeness and in His own image.